Child Labour in Ind

CW00880629

Kaur

ective

Rajinder Kaur

Child Labour in India: A National and International Perspective

LAP LAMBERT Academic Publishing

Impressum / Imprint

Bibliografische Information der Deutschen Nationalbibliothek: Die Deutsche Nationalbibliothek verzeichnet diese Publikation in der Deutschen Nationalbibliografie; detaillierte bibliografische Daten sind im Internet über http://dnb.d-nb.de abrufbar.
Alle in diesem Buch genannten Marken und Produktnamen unterliegen warenzeichen-, marken- oder patentrechtlichem Schutz bzw. sind Warenzeichen oder eingetragene Warenzeichen der jeweiligen Inhaber. Die Wiedergabe von Marken, Produktnamen, Gebrauchsnamen, Handelsnamen, Warenbezeichnungen u.s.w. in diesem Werk berechtigt auch ohne besondere Kennzeichnung nicht zu der Annahme, dass solche Namen im Sinne der Warenzeichen- und Markenschutzgesetzgebung als frei zu betrachten wären und daher von jedermann benutzt werden dürften.

Bibliographic information published by the Deutsche Nationalbibliothek: The Deutsche Nationalbibliothek lists this publication in the Deutsche Nationalbibliografie; detailed bibliographic data are available in the Internet at http://dnb.d-nb.de.
Any brand names and product names mentioned in this book are subject to trademark, brand or patent protection and are trademarks or registered trademarks of their respective holders. The use of brand names, product names, common names, trade names, product descriptions etc. even without a particular marking in this works is in no way to be construed to mean that such names may be regarded as unrestricted in respect of trademark and brand protection legislation and could thus be used by anyone.

Coverbild / Cover image: www.ingimage.com

Verlag / Publisher:
LAP LAMBERT Academic Publishing
ist ein Imprint der / is a trademark of
OmniScriptum GmbH & Co. KG
Heinrich-Böcking-Str. 6-8, 66121 Saarbrücken, Deutschland / Germany
Email: info@lap-publishing.com

Herstellung: siehe letzte Seite /
Printed at: see last page
ISBN: 978-3-659-61997-7

CHILD LABOUR IN INDIA:
A NATIONAL AND INTERNATIONAL PERSPECTIVE

Dr. Rajinder Kaur

Assistant Professor, Department of Laws

Panjab University, Chandigarh

India

Preface

"Every child when born brings with the hope that god is not yet disappointed with man" stated Rabindra Nath Tagore. These words itself recognize the fact that all children constitute the most fundamental and valuable resource of any society. But unfortunately being vulnerable in nature they are often subjected to various kinds of exploitation. Millions of children have no access to education, work for long hours in various types of hazardous and non-hazardous occupation for survival, forced to become child soldiers and are subjected to problems like sexual abuse, violence, trafficking. They are deprived of healthy nutritious diet and right to play. At the age when they should be in school, majority of poor children of a lesser god work hard. In the, post-independence era, India has experienced an unequivocal expression of commitment of the government to the cause of children. The Constitution of India itself and several other legislations clearly depicts the intention of the legislators. But in practice only lip service is being paid to these legislations due to apathetic social attitude in general and bureaucratic inertia in particular. There is a need to change the approach of government and the society as a whole to accept children as a partners and active participant in creating a culture of children rights.

To understand the various aspects of child rights, the present research is carried out in order to deliver one message that in the era of globalization, there is an urgent need to change the mindset of both government and the adult citizens with regard to children, the adults of tomorrow. Children of today are to be given due respect and their dignity should be protected by ensuring complete protection of their rights, which is essential for their all round development, only then they can be called as true torchbearers of the future world order.

TABLE OF CONTENTS

CHAPTER I
INTRODUCTION

The question of child's rights has emerged as one of the most vibrant issues for discussion in this new millennium. The fact remains that even today children are a part of the disadvantaged minority group so far as realization of human rights and social justice are concerned. The main reason for this lacuna is that children are still not a complete political entity in true sense of the term. Besides, they are generally physically, mentally and economically defenseless. In this rapidly changing age of globalization, taking care of child's right at every stage has taken a back seat. This not only affects the whole value system, but also their present social and economic needs. No doubt that the future of humanity depends on children to a large extent, even then a very partial and parochial approach has been followed towards bringing them on the mainstream of social and political agenda.

This marginalization takes even a much worse turn when child is either orphan, loner, a destitute, a homeless, a child labour, a bonded labour, a domestic help, a street child, a physically or a mentally challenged child. In such circumstances, they remain mostly in uncared state and became highly vulnerable to crimes which are perpetrated against them. Violations of *Child Rights* are hooked to social wrong. It ranges from actual crimes to neglect by society and unsatisfactory parenting, innocence, inexperience, wrong exposure, improper care, lack of good guidance and non existence of good social security system are some of the major reasons for children's continued vulnerability and exploitation.

The children are the greatest gift of God to man, our most precious and important assets. The welfare and development of any community depends largely on the health and well being of its children. It has been said 'who hold souls of the children holds the nation'.[1] The physical and mental health of a nation is determined largely in the manner in which it is shaped in early stages. Justice V.R. Krishna Iyer says that it is our obligation to the generation by opening up all opportunities for every child to unfold its personality and rise to its full stature physical, moral, mental and spiritual and it is the birth right of every child that cries for justice from the world as a whole.[2] During World War-II Winston Churchill said "there is no finer investment for any community than putting milk into babies." This appeal to the people everywhere, this fundamental faith in Juvenile Justice, this reorganization of the worth of the infants born and unborn, is the beginning of Juvenile Justice, says Justice Krishna Iyer.[3] The needs and rights of children should not be attended as bye-product of progress. They should be attended as an end and means of progress. Unless this change is achieved all investments in food, production, community service and human resources development would remain less effective because children constitutes a significant proportion of the people and they will not be able to contribute fully to them nor benefited fully from them. We must not forget that the children are the ultimate goal for development. We must also realize that the efforts for advance in human conditions must start as early as possible beginning with the child and the mother well-being even before the child is born. Protecting the health and education of today's children is not only the first and foremost right but also is the most basic and wisest of all investments in social and economic development of society.[4]

The child of today cannot develop to be a responsible and productive member of tomorrow's society unless an environment which is conducive to social and physical health is assured to him. Every nation, developed or developing, links its future with the states of the child. Children are the greatest gift to the humanity. The parents themselves live for them. Parents regain peace and happiness in the company

---

[1] Shriniwas Gupta, *Rights of Child and Child Labour: A Critical Study*,JILI, XXXVII,(1995),p.531.
[2] V.R. Krishna Iyer, *Jurisprudence of Juvenile Justice: A Preambular Perspective.* Quoted in *Supra* note 1.
[3] *Ibid.*
[4] Karl-Eric *'Key note address National Seminar on the rights on the child: Socio-legal perspective'*, 15-16 September, 1990.

of the children. The children signify eternal optimism in the human being and always provide the potential for human development. If the children are better equipped with a broader human output, the society will feel happy with them. Neglecting the children means loss to the society as a whole. If children are deprived of their childhood - socially, economically, physically, mentally - the nations get deprived of the potential human resources for social progress, economic empowerment and peace and order, the social stability and good citizenry.[5] It may be that the aforesaid appeal lies at the back of the saying that "child is the father of man". To enable fathering of a valiant and vibrant man, the child must be groomed well in the formative years of his life. He must receive education, acquire knowledge of man and materials and blossom in such an atmosphere that on reaching age, he is found to be a man with a mission, a man who matters so far as the society is concerned.[6]

Childhood is a universal human experience and every society has a vital stake in it children. The future and stability of a society depend on the quality of its children. Infact, in every child the foundation of a nation is laid. The proper development of the child is, therefore, imperative for the proper growth of a nation. This applies to the international community also. Obviously Child Welfare is of supreme importance to the mankind. Child Welfare is an expression which means "the general well being of the child. In all ages this has depended principally on the social valuation of children and the care accorded to them. At the present time the child is considered as an important social unit and is held to be entitled to all that makes for healthy living, sufficient recreation, schooling adapted to his natural learning methods, intelligent home care and the right to develop his abilities to their fullest extent".[7] The expression refers to "the total well-being of the child. It includes not only the care of maladjusted and delinquent children but also the development of

[5] Bandhua Mukti Morcha etc. v. Union of India and others AIR 1997 SC 2218, p. 2220.
[6] M.C. Mehta v. State of Tamil Nadu and others, AIR 1997 SC 701.
[7] Edwin R.A. Seligman, Editor-in-Chief, *Encyclopedia of the Social Sciences, Vol-III,* (Macmillan Company, 1951 reprint), p.380.

child physical, mental, emotional and social faculties.[8] In nutshell, it 'emphasizes the need of continuously taking into account all aspects of the child's well-being and dealing with 'the whole child', not some isolated phase of his development".[9] The intense realizations, that what the best and wisest parent wants for his own child, that must the community want for all its children.

Child care and welfare, traditionally the exclusive responsibility of family and kin, is now shared by the State in an increasing number of countries. Obligation for child's care and welfare are being less left to traditional precept and custom, and increasingly placed under larger legal scrutiny and social legislation. This is shown by the ways in which nations have established norms and regulation for child welfare, without unduly encroaching upon the independence and privacy of individual and familial rights. The statement of objects and reasons appended to the Central Children Act, 1960 emphasize the importance and protection of children.[10]

> *Children are the most vulnerable group in any population and in need of the greatest social care. On account of their vulnerability and dependence they can be exploited, ill-treated and directed into undesirable channels by anti-social element in the community. The state has the duty of according proper care and protection to children at all times.*

It is needless to emphasize that children are a nation's strength and most important assets. Every year since 1957, 14th November is being observed in India as Children's Day. The day, coinciding with the birthday of India's First Prime Minister Sh. Jawahar Lal Nehru, inspires us to focus our undivided attention towards the basic needs and rights of children, so that their well being becomes our prime concern. India's population of young comprises nearly 380 million children below the age of

---

[8] Alice Jacob and Kusum Kumar *'Child Welfare'*, S.N. Jain, Ed. *'Child and the law'* (N.M. Tripathi, 1979), p.41.
[9] *Ibid.*
[10] See, the object and Reasons appended to the Children Act, 1960. The Preamble to the Act of 1960 puts the same theme thus:
An Act to provide for the care, protection, maintenance, welfare, training education and rehabilitation of neglected or delinquent children.

14 years as per 2001 census.[11] The status of children, who represent nearly 40% of the 'Human Capital' of India, not only reflects the quality of life of people in the country, but also measures its Human Development Index. The Government considers the development of children as its key concern and firmly believes that in the ultimate analysis, it is childhood that holds potential and sets the limits for the future development of society. Today investing in the requirements and priorities of children is considered to be the sine qua-non of a developed nation.

---

[11] Asha Bajpai, *Child Rights in India: Law, Policy and Practice,* (Oxford University Press, New Delhi, 2003), p.1.

CHAPTER II
CHILD RIGHTS AND INTERNATIONAL FRAMEWORK

We are guilty of many errors and many faults, but our worst crime is
abandoning the children, neglecting the fountain of life. Many of the
things we need could perhaps wait; but the cause of the child cannot.
Right now is the time his bones are being formed, his blood being made
and his sense being developed. To him, we cannot answer 'Tomorrow',
His name is 'Today'.

(Gabriel Mitral) [1]

Both at National and International level great interest is being shown in the matter of welfare of children. Englantyne Jebbs of England was the first person to initiate the international movement for providing the child with a status. The debates, she initiated culminated in Declaration adopted by League of Nations[2] on September 26, 1925.[3] It can be seen as the first International instrument dealing with children's right. The five principles that was enumerated were:

- The child must be given the means requisite for its normal development, both materially and spiritually.
- The child that is hungry must be fed; the child that is sick must be nursed; the child that is backward must be helped; the delinquent must be reclaimed; and the orphan must be sheltered.
- The child must be first to receive relief in the time of distress.
- The child must be in a position to earn a livelihood and must be protected against every form of exploitation.

---

[1] Quoted by V.R. Krishna Iyer in *'Law and Life'*, (Vikas Publishing House Pvt. Ltd., Ghaziabad, 1979), p.8.
[2] League of Nations conceived during First World War established in 1919 under the Treaty of Versailles to promote International Co-operation and to achieve peace and security.
[3] Dolly Singh, *Child Rights and Social Wrongs Volume-II., Child is a Global citizen: A Third World perspective*, (Kansiksha Publishers, Distributors, New Delhi), 2001, p.48.

- The child must be brought up in the consciousness that its talents must be devoted to the service of its fellow men.

This Declaration is important as it highlights the social and economic entitlement of children and establishes internationally the concept of the rights of the child, thereby laying the foundation for setting future international standard in the field of children rights.[4] But unfortunately the declaration could not give effect as the league itself died and in 1944, it was replaced by another international organization, the UN.

2.1. Role of United Nations

During Second World War, 26 Nations pledged to continue fighting together against the axis powers, United Nation came into existence on 24th October, 1945.[5] The focal object of the organization was maintenance of international peace and security. Later on this organization started working for the rights of Human beings i.e. Human Rights and in 1948 the Universal Declaration on Human Rights was adopted,[6] and this Bible of Rights also specifies rights provided to the child. Article 25(2) specifically provides special care and protection to children which read as:

Article 25(2) of the UDHR provides that Mother and Childhood are entitled
to special care and assistance, all children whether born in or out of
wedlock shall enjoy special protection.
Article 26 of the UDHR provides for education of children.

2.1.1.   Declaration on the Rights of Child, 1959

It was only in fifties of the twentieth century that the separate charter on the rights of the child was declared. It was unanimously adopted by U.N. General

---

[4] Geraldine Van Bueren, *The International Law on the Rights of the Child,* (Netherland: Kluwer Academic Publishers, 1995).
[5] On 1st Jan, 1942 U.S. President Franklin D. Roosevett coined the name United Nations.
[6] <http://www.unhchr.ch/udhr/lang/eng.htm> accessed on 20th December, 2013.

Assembly on 20th November, 1959. The preamble describes the principle as enunciating rights and freedom of child which governments should observe by legislative and other measures progressively taken. It re-iterates the pledge that 'mankind owes to the child the best it has to give', and it places a specific duty upon voluntary organization and local authorities to strive for the observance of these rights. The declaration provides:[7]

a)   The child by reasons of his physical and mental immaturity needs special safeguard and case including appropriate legal protection.

b)   The child shall enjoy special benefits of security.

c)   The child shall enjoy protection and shall be given opportunities and facilities by law and by all other means to develop in a health and normal manner and in condition of freedom and dignity.

In the enactment of Law for this purpose:

a)   The best interest of child shall be of paramount consideration.

b)   The General Assembly calls upon local authorities and national Government to recognize these rights and strive for their observance.

c)   All children without any exception whatsoever shall be entitled to these rights, without distinction or discrimination on account of national or social origin, poverty, both or status.

There was a remarkable departure from the principles laid down in 1925 Declaration. Whereas, the earlier Declaration specified that 'children must be the first to receive relief, the 1959 Declaration lays down that children shall be 'among the first' to receive protection and relief and are entitled to 'special protection'. The Declaration also contains a broad non-discrimination clause.

---

[7] <http://www.unhchr.ch/html/menu 3/b/25.htm> accessed on 18th December, 2013.

2.1.2.   International Covenant on Civil and Political Rights, 1966 (ICCPR)

Under the ICCPR, 1966[8] which complements the Economic, Social and Cultural covenants, children are implicitly entitled to the benefit from all relevant rights contained in the covenant and in addition there are specific provisions for children. Article 14(1) provides an express exception to the right to a hearing in a public, when it is in the interest of juveniles or where it concerns the guardianship of children. According to Article 14(3) (f) of the covenant the criminal proceeding should take account of juvenile's age and their desirability of promoting their rehabilitation. Article 10(3) provides an obligation to states parties to separate accused juveniles from accused adults and bring them as speedily as possible for adjudication and accord them treatment according to their age and legal status.

Under the said covenant, the family is recognized as being the natural and fundamental unit of the society and as such is entitled to State Protection[9]. The State parties are further obliged to respect the liberty of parents to ensure the religious and moral education of children in accordance with their beliefs and in the event of dissolution of the marriage; provision shall be made for the protection of any children[10]. In addition to the protection of child ICCPR incorporates a specific provision on children in Article 24[11] which embodies following:

1.   Every child shall have, without any discrimination as to race, colour, sex, language, religion, national or social origin, property or birth, the right to such measures of protection as are required by his status as a minor, on the part of his family, society and the State.

2.   Every child shall be registered immediately after birth and shall have a name.

3.   Every child has the right to acquire a nationality.

---

[8] <http://www.umn.edu/humanrts/instree/b3 ccpr.htm> accessed on 18th December, 2013.
[9] *Article 23*, ICCPR, 1966.
[10] *Article 18(4) and 24(4)*, ICCPR, 1966.
[11] *Article 24*, ICCPR, 1966.

2.1.3. Convention on the Rights of the Child, 1989

The widespread plight of children attracted the attention of United Nations. In December 1976, the United Nations adopted a resolution which proclaimed 1979 as an International year of the child. In the consequence, the Government of Poland submitted a draft on the rights of the child for adoption by the UN General Assembly as a lasting memorial year of the child. After a revised version and a decade campaigning, the UN General Assembly adopted the Convention on the Rights of Child[12] on November 20th, 1976 ratified by 135 nations including India.

The said convention on the Rights of the child is a United Nations agreement that spells out the range of rights that children everywhere are entitled to. It sets basic standards for children's well being at different stages of their development. Countries that ratify the convention agree that they be legally bound by its provisions. They report regularly to an expert Committee on the Rights of the Child as to steps they have taken to comply with the provisions of the Convention.

The Convention is the first legally binding code of *Child Rights* in history. It brings together in one treaty all the relevant *Child Rights* issue, rather than having them scattered among a number of international treaties. The Convention on the *Child Rights* contains 54 articles, each of which entails a different type of right. These can be broken down into four broad categories.

Survival Rights	:	Cover child's rights to life and the needs that are most basic to existence; these include an adequate living standard, shelter, nutrition and access to medical services.
Developmental Rights	:	Include those things that children require in order to reach their fullest potential. Examples are right to education, play and leisure, cultural activities, access to information,

[12] <http://www.unhchr.ch/html/menu 2/6 crc/treaties/crc.htm> accessed on 15th December, 2012.

		freedom of thought expression, conscience and religion.
Protection Rights	:	Require that children be safeguarded against all forms of abuse, neglect and exploitation. They cover issues such as special care for refugee children, torture, abuses in the criminal justice system, involvement in armed conflict, child labour, drug abuse and sexual exploitation.
Participation Rights	:	Allow children to take an active role in their communities and nations. These encompass the freedom to express opinions, to have a say in matters affecting their own lives, to join associations and to assemble peacefully. As their abilities develop, children are to have increasing opportunities to participate in the activities of their society, in preparation for responsible adult hood.

The UN Committee on the Rights of Child has identified a thematic clustering of *Child Rights*. This clustering is as follows:[13]

- *Definition of Child:* Article 16 provides that for the purpose of the present convention a child means every human being below the age of eighteen years unless under the law applicable to the child majority is attained earlier.[14]

- *General measures of implementation* are laid down in Articles 4, 44 of Convention on the Rights of Child. This highlights the need to constantly review the relevance of reservations and the importance of bringing national legislation in conformity with the Convention.[15]

---

[13] Asha Bajpai, *Child Rights in India: Law, Policy and Practice,* (Oxford University Press, New Delhi, 2003), pp. 18-19.
[14] *Ibid.*
[15] *Ibid.*

- *General principles, Civil Rights and Freedoms:* In this theme Article 2, 3, 6 and 12 of the Convention give the four general principles i.e. non-discrimination, best interests of the child, right to survival and development and respect for the views of the child. Articles 7, 8, 13-17 and 37(a) specify the civil rights and freedom which include the right to a name and nationality, freedom of expression and peaceful assembly, right against torture etc.[16]

- *The Rights relating to family environment and basic health* are covered under Article 5, 9-11, 18, 19, 21, 25 and 27 that deal with parental guidance and responsibilities, illicit transfer and non-return, un-accompanied minors and adoption, psychological recovery and re-integration. It also includes articles that address health, standard of living and facilities for treatment and rehabilitation under Articles 6, 18, 23, 24, 26 & 27.[17]

- *The theme on education, leisure and special protection* stresses the importance of education including, vocational training and guidance and also protection of refugee children, children in emergencies, children in the juvenile justice system, and children in danger of exploitation. In Article 28, 29 and 31, it is laid down that education should be child friendly. Physical and psychological recovery as well as social integration for children is given under Article 22, 32-36 and 37-40.[18]

The convention is derived from a core set of human value that recognize the inherent dignity and the equal and inalienable rights of all members of the human family as the foundation of freedom, justice and peace in world. There are also four general principles laid down in the convention. These four principles are:-

1. *Non Discrimination (Article 2):* State Parties must ensure that all children within their jurisdiction enjoy their rights. No child should

---

[16] *Ibid.*
[17] *Ibid.*
[18] *Ibid.*

suffer from discrimination, Refugee children, children with disabilities, children of foreign origin or minority group should have the same rights as all others.

2. *Best Interests of the Child (Article 3):* When the authorities of a State take decisions which affect children, the best interests of the children must be the primary consideration. The principle relates to decisions by courts of law, administrative authorities legislative bodies and both public and private social welfare institutions.

3. *The Right to Life Survival and Development (Article 6):* The term development in this context should be interpreted in a broad sense, adding a qualitative dimension not only physical health but also mental, emotional, cognitive, social and cultural development.

4. *The view of the Child (Article 12):* Children have the right to be heard and to have their views taken seriously, including any judicial or administrative proceedings affecting them[19].

The Convention thus constitutes a radical departure from previous practices where the rights of the child were found scattered and lacking global consensus. The convention for the first time incorporates all rights into one single comprehensive document whose provisions are meant to be applied globally. It appears that children by virtue of the fact that they are humans are entitled to the rights enjoyed by the adults.

2.1.4. Regional Instruments for the protection of Child Rights

Recognizing that the each region had its own peculiar concerns, the Council of Europe, the Organization of American States (OAS) and Organization of African

---

[19] *Ibid,* p.20.

Unity (OAU) has adopted provisions for the protection of *Child Rights* in their respective instruments.

Subsequently, the rights of child has also been reaffirmed in the World Conference on Education for All at Jomtien Declaration in March 1990; World Summit on the children in the Autumn of 1990, SAARC Conference on children in 1991 and 1992. In 1998 in an annual Summit of SAARC celebrating the 50th Anniversary year of the UN Universal Declaration on Human Rights, Amnesty International said "South Asian Governments should mark this anniversary by taking concrete actions to improve the lives of the regions children, rather than making another round of unfulfilled promises.[20] They further added that child's rights should be placed at the counter of their agenda; if they are really committed to do a better future for the region.

2.2. Role of ILO

Born from the chaos of global War, tempered by nearly a century of turbulent change, the International Labour Organization (ILO) is built on the constitutional principle that universal and lasting peace can be established only if it is based on social justice. The ILO came into existence on 11 April, 1919 after First World War, following the treaty of Versailles. In recognition of its work it was awarded Noble Peace Prize in 1969.

The ILO[21] is a unique among all the UN Organizations due to its tripartite structure; that is both the employees and the workers representatives – the social partners of the economy have an equal voice with those of governments in shaping its policies and programmes. The ILO encourages tripartism within the member States too, by promoting social dialogue that involves trade unions and the employees in the formulation and, where appropriate, in implementation of the national policy on

---

[20] *SAARC Leaders: Make Child Rights a Priority*; Amensty International, Legal News and Views, September, 1998.
[21] For details see <http://www.ilo.org> accessed on 10th December, 2013.

social and economic affairs. There are currently 175 members states of ILO. A Governing Body comprising 28 government members 14 workers, and 14 employees members guides the work of ILO. The International Labour Conference meets annually and provides the forum for discussion of world's labour and social problems. The ILO's technical co-operation is focused on four major areas which correspond to its strategic objectives:

- Promote and realize fundamental principles and rights at work.
- Create greater opportunities for women and men to secure decent employment.
- Enhance the coverage and effectiveness of social protection for all.
- Strengthen tripartism and social dialogue.

In India, the ILO services and activities have focused on strengthening the capacity of the trade unions and employers to address the issues emerging from the economic reforms- industrial restructing, social security systems and reforms in industrial relations. ILO has also sought to support workers education and training activities in the fields of collective bargaining, occupational safety, health and environment, leadership training, contract labour, international labour standards, women's participation in trade unions and organizing the unorganized in the informal or rural sector. The ILO's mission today is to promote decent work for all in the global economy – in conditions of freedom, equality, security and human dignity. It does through permanent contact with workers, employees and governments, helping forge new and innovative employment, labour market and training policies. Concern for the social costs of globalization increases the need for better international co-ordination of macroeconomics policies to diminish its harmful consequences. The ILO believe that the observance of fundamental principles and rights at work are the cornerstone for any socially sustainable economic development process. ILO has adopted some of the important conventions and recommendations concerning child labour which   both prohibit the employment of children and set basic standards and conditions under which children above certain age may be permitted to work in different sectors of employment.

2.2.1.   Conventions Adopted by ILO

Minimum Age (Industry) Conventions, 1919 (No.5)[22] and

Minimum Age (Industry) Convention, (Revised) 1937 (No.59)[23]

Convention No.5 of 1919 prohibits the employment of children under the age of 14 years in 'Industrial Undertaking', other than an undertaking in which the members of the same family are employed. The term 'Industrial undertaking' includes mines, quarries, manufacturing industries, construction, maintenance, repairs, transport of passengers or goods by road or rail or inland waterway.

India has already ratified this Convention and prohibition of employment of Children below 14 years has been statutorily implemented through the Factories Act, 1948.[24]

The above Convention was, however, revised in 1937 by Convention No.59, raising the minimum age for employment, of children in industrial undertaking from 14 to 15 years. The revised Convention also imposed a restriction on employment of children below 15 years of age even in industrial undertaking in which only members of the employer's family are employed provided that such employment is dangerous to the life, health and morals of the children employed. It has also been provided that medical certificate shall be necessary for such children employed in mines etc.

Though some relaxation's have been made for India, yet it has not been able to ratify this Convention so far, obviously because the Factories Act, 1948 still prescribes 14 years as the minimum age for employment of children in factories.

---

[22] <http://www.ilo.org/ilolex/cgi-lex/convde.pl?C005> accessed on 20th December, 2013.

[23] <http://www.ilo.org/ilolex/cgi-lex/convde.pl?C059> accessed on 20th December, 2013.

[24] Section 67 of Factories Act, 1948 provides: Prohibition of Employment of Young Children – No child who has not completed his fourteenth year shall be required or allowed to work in any factory.

Minimum Age (Non-Industrial Employment) Convention, 1932 (No.33), and Minimum Age (Non-Industrial Employment) Convention (Revised), No.60 of 1937 raised the minimum age for admission to employment in non-industrial employment from 14 to 15 years. Special provisions have been made for India. The Revised Convention provides that children under 13 years of age are not to be employed in non-industrial occupations such as shops, office, hotels or restaurants, places of public entertainments. However, national laws may permit the appearance of children below the age of 13 years in the interest of art, science or education. Further, person under 17 years of age shall not be employed in non-industrial employment's which involve danger to life, health or morals.

India has not so far ratified any of the Conventions. The minimum age prescribed by the different state enactments for employment of children varies from 12 to 14 years. Further there is no provision in these statutes with regard to the minimum age for hazardous employment.[25]

Minimum Age (Sea) Convention, 1920 (No.7)[26] and

Minimum Age (Sea) Convention (Revised), 1936 (No.58)[27]

The Convention No.7 of 1920 prohibits the employment of children under the age of 14 years on vessels (ships and boats engaged in maritime navigation), other than vessels upon which only members of the same family are employed. However, on revision of the Convention in 1936, the minimum age for admission to employment was raised from 14 to 15 years. However, national laws may provide for the issue in respect of age permitting them to be employed in cases which an educational or other appropriate authority is satisfied, after having due regard to the health and physical condition of the child, that such employment will be beneficial to

---

[25] Shops and Commercial Establishment Act, 1969. Minimum age of employment is 12 years in Bihar, Gujarat, J&K, Madhya Pradesh, Karnataka, Orissa, Rajasthan, Tripura, Uttar Pradesh, West Bengal, Goa, Daman & Div & Manipur. Minimum age is 14 years in Andhra Pradesh, Assam, Haryana, Himachal Pradesh, Tamil Nadu, Kerala, Punjab, Delhi, Chandigarh, Pondichery and Megalaya. Minimum age of employment is 15 years in Maharastra.

[26] <http://www.ilo.org/ilolex/cgi-lex/convde.pl?C007>accessed on 20th December, 2013.

[27] <http://www.ilo.org/ilolex/cgi-lex/convde.pl?C058> accessed on 20th December, 2013.

him.

India has not ratified these Conventions. As a sizable number of Indian Seamen are employed on foreign ships, mostly British, ratification by India would not be of advantage to a large majority of Indian seamen until the United Kingdom also agrees to ratify.

Minimum Age (Trimmers and Stokers) Convention, 1921 (No.15)[28]

The Convention prohibits the employment of young persons under 18 yeas of age as Trimmers or Stokers on vessels engaged in maritime navigation. But an exception has been made with regard to India by lowering the minimum age from 18 to 15 years if found physically fit after medical examination. India has ratified this Convention and its provisions have been fully implemented through the Merchant Shipping Act, 1958.[29]

Minimum Age (Fishermen) Convention, 1959 (No.112)[30]

The Convention provides that children under the age of 15 years shall not be employed on fishing vessels (ships and boats engaged in salt water). However, such children may occasionally take part in the activities on board fishing vessels during school holidays for noncommercial purposes. Further, it has also been provided that the national laws may permit children of not less than 14 years of age to be employed in cases in which educational or appropriate authority is satisfied, having due regard to the health and physical condition and the benefits to the child from employment, that such employment will be beneficial to the child. India has neither ratified this Convention so far nor enacted any law to regulate employment of children on fishing vessels.

Minimum Age (Agriculture) Convention, 1921 (No.10)[31]

---

[28] <http://www.ilo.org/ilolex/cgi-lex/convde.pl?C015> accessed on 20th December, 2013.
[29] Section 109 & 110 of Merchant Shipping Act, 1958.
[30] <http://www.ilo.org/ilolex/cgi-lex/convde.pl?C112> accessed on 20th December, 2013.
[31] <http://www.ilo.org/ilolex/cgi-lex/convde.pl?C010> accessed on 20th December, 2013.

The Convention provides that children under the age of 14 years shall not be employed or work in any public or private agricultural undertakings, save outside the hours fixed for school attendance. If they are employed outside school hours, the employment shall not be such as to prejudice their attendance at schools. The children may however be employed for purposes of practical vocational instructions subject to certain restrictions. Similarly, the prohibition of employment of children in agriculture does not apply if they work in technical schools approved and supervised by public authority.

The Convention has not so far been ratified by India, obviously keeping in view the difficulties in implementing its provisions effectively over vast unorganized agriculture activities.

Minimum Age (Underground Work) Convention, 1965 (No.123)[32]

Though the Minimum Age (Industry) Convention (Revised) 1937 (No.59) prohibits employment of children under the age of 15 years, which applies to mines as well as the Convention No.123 of 1965 prescribes 16 years of age for employment of children underground in mines.   India has not only ratified the Convention but also incorporated its provisions in the Mines Act, 1952.[33]

Minimum Age Convention, 1973 (No.138)[34]

This is a general Convention fixing the minimum age for employment, which will gradually replace the existing Conventions on the subject limited to particular economic sectors. The idea is to achieve total abolition of child labour. It calls for the pursuit of a national policy designed to ensure the effective abolition of child labour and for raising progressively the minimum age for admission to employment or work to a level consistent with the fullest physical and mental development of young

---

[32] <http://www.ilo.org/ilolex/cgi-lex/convde.pl?C123> accessed on 20th December, 2013.
[33] Section 11 of Mines Act, 1952.
[34] <http://www.ilo.org/ilolex/cgi-lex/convde.pl?C138> accessed on 20th December, 2013.

persons. The minimum age provided under the Convention is not to be less than the age of completion of compulsory schooling and, in any case, not less than 15 years. Developing countries may, however, initially fix the minimum age at 14 years. In the case of work, which is likely to jeopardize the health, safety or morals of young persons, it has been stipulated that the minimum age should not be less than 18 years. The Convention is applicable, as a minimum to mining, quarrying, manufacturing units, construction, plantation, and other agricultural undertaking producing for commercial purpose.

India has not yet ratified the Convention. The present Indian laws do not conform to the standards laid down by the Convention in several respects. Firstly, there is no law fixing any minimum age for employment in agriculture. Even in case of plantations the age fixed is 12 years.[35] Secondly, though the Child Labour (Prohibition & Regulation Act, 1986 deals with employment of children in hazardous employment, yet the minimum age fixed is lower than that laid down in the Convention. Thirdly, the Factories Act, 1948 fixes the minimum age of employment at 14[36] whereas the Convention fixes it at 15. Fourthly, in case of non-industrial employment the various state enactments have fixed the minimum age varying from 12 to 14 years and therefore, our laws are deficit in that respect also.

2.2.2.   Recommendations of ILO

Minimum   Age   (Non-Industrial   Employment)   Recommendation,   1932 (No.41)[37]

This Recommendation lays down a higher standard than the two Conventions on the subject. It envisages that so long as the children are required to attend school, their employment should be restricted as far as possible. Even for employment of children in light work outside school hours, the consent of the parents or guardian

---

[35] Section 24, The Plantation Labour Act, 1951.
[36] Section 67, The Factories Act, 1948.
[37] <http://www.ilo.org/ilolex/cgi-lex/convde.pl?R041> accessed on 20th December, 2012.

should be obtained and there should be a medical certificate of fitness for employment.

Minimum Age (Family Undertakings), Recommendations, 1937 (No.52)[38]

The Recommendation requires that member-states should extent their legislation on minimum age for the admission of children to industrial work, to those also who are employed in family undertakings.[39]

Minimum Age (Coal Mines) Recommendations, 1953 (No.96)[40]

The Recommendations; embodies the principles that young persons under the age of 16 years should not be employed underground in coal-mines.

Minimum Age (Underground Work) Recommendation, 1965 (No.124)[41]

The Recommendation requires that where the minimum age for admission to employment underground in mines is less than 16 years, steps should be taken as speedily as possible to raise it to that level. Further it should be progressively raised, with a view to attain a minimum age of 18 years.

Minimum Age Recommendation, 1973 (No.146)[42]

Besides emphasizing the measure required to be adopted for overall development of child labour, it recommends that the minimum age should be fixed at the same level for all sectors of economic activity. Member-states should progressively raise the minimum age of employment to 16 years and where it is still below 15 years to raise it to the level. Where it is not possible to fix a minimum age for all employment in agriculture and other related activities in rural areas. It should

---

[38] <http://www.ilo.org/ilolex/cgi-lex/convde.pl?R052> accessed on 20th December, 2012.
[39] Proviso to Section 3 of The Child Labour (Prohibition and Regulation) Act, 1986 provides that prohibition of employment is not applicable where process is carried on by an occupier with the aid of his family or school established by or recognized or receiving assistance from Government. Therefore, the Act itself legalizes the employment in family undertakings.
[40] <http://www.ilo.org/ilolex/cgi-lex/convde.pl?R096> accessed on 20th December, 2012.
[41] <http://www.ilo.org/ilolex/cgi-lex/convde.pl?R124> accessed on 20th December, 2012.
[42] <http://www.ilo.org/ilolex/cgi-lex/convde.pl?R146> accessed on 20th December, 2013.

at least be fixed for plantations and other commercial crops. For hazardous employment immediate steps should be taken to raise the minimum age to 18 years.

Unicef[43] -UK has created a series of leaflets aimed at helping British Businesses discourage child labour in countries-where they invest. The leaflets, entitled 'Basic facts for business', deal with child labour in 10 specific countries. They are designed to inform the companies about how children become part of the workforce, the size of the problem, the legal situation in each country and practical steps that companies can take to end child labour. The countries covered are India Bangladesh, United Kingdom, Brazil, Nepal, Thailand, EL Salvador, Pakistan, Costa Rica and Tanzania. The President of the Confederation of British Industry (CBI), Sir Colin Marshal said that "British industry has a responsibility to the world's children to make sure the products we sell are not in any way exploiting children or denying them their rights".[44]

The Optional Protocol on the involvement of children in the armed conflicts raises the age of recruitment to armed forces from 15 to 18. The optional protocol on the sale of children, child prostitution and pornography focuses on the criminalisation of these violations of children's rights, while emphasizing the need for increased public awareness and international co-operation in efforts to combat them. The recognition and implementation of children's rights are the bedrock measures of our progress as a civilization.   The United States became one of the first countries to sign United Nations two key protocols that strengthen global standards for the protection of children. The signing of the protocols by the, former US President Clinton, was warmly welcomed by UN officials involved in efforts to protect children. Welcoming the US leader ship in signing the key optional protocols to the convention on the rights of the child on protecting children against prostitution and

---

[43] Unicef – United Nations Children's Emergency Fund – an organization created in 1946 to provide massive emergency relief to the destitute of the young victims of 2nd World War. It also provides assistance to the flood and cyclone victims in India and Pakistan.

[44] UK- The facts about Child Labour, April 29, 1998. www.bbc.com accessed on 20th December, 2012.

involvement in armed conflict. Carol Bellamy Executive Director of UNICEF and Louise Frechettee, Deputy Secretary-General of UN say that the move would undoubtedly inspire other countries to add their names to these instruments.[45]

2.2.3.   Worst forms of Child Labour Convention, 1999

Recently, adopted Convention No.182[46] and an accompanying Recommendation No.190[47] calls upon the governments to ban and take immediate steps for the elimination of the worst forms of Child Labour[48]. Members State of the ILO, on 17th June, 1999 took a decisive step towards saving million of children around the world from the worst forms of hazardous and exploitative work. The new convention, which will apply to all children under the age of 18, calls for countries to prohibit and eliminate the worst forms of child labour as matter of urgency. For the first time, the treaty defines, what constitutes exploitative practices-such as slavery, debt bondage and child prostitution-include a ban on forced recruitment of child soldier.

Article 1 of the convention provides that each member who ratifies this convention shall take immediate measures to secure the prohibition and elimination of worst forms of child labour as a matter of urgency. For the purpose of this convention, the term 'worst form of child labour' comprises:[49]

a)   All forms of slavery & practices similar to slavery, such as sale and trafficking of children, debt bondage and serfdom and forced or compulsory labour including forced or compulsory recruitment of children for use in armed conflict;

b)   The use, procuring or offering of a child for prostitution, for the production of pornography or for pornographic performances;

---

[45] UN New letter, 19th June, 1999.
[46] <http://www.ilo.org/ilolex/cgi-lex/convde.pl?C182> accessed on 20th December, 2013.
[47] <http://www.ilo.org/ilolex/cgi-lex/convde.pl?R190> accessed on 20th December, 2013.
[48] UN News Letters, 19th June, 1999.
[49] *Article 3,* Worst form of Child Labour Convention, 1999.

c)   The use, procuring or offering of a child for illicit activities, in particular for the production and trafficking or drugs as defined in the relevant international treaties;

d)   Work which, by its nature or the circumstances in which it is carried out, is likely to harm the health, safety or morals of children.

Three other new international instruments were adopted dealing specifically with some of the issues defined as among the worst forms of child labour, namely:

- The Optional Protocol to the Convention on the Rights of the Child on the involvement of children in Armed Conflict (OPAC).[50]
- The Optional Protocol to the Convention of Rights of Child on the Sale of Children, Child Prostitution and Child Pornography (OPSC).
- The Protocol to prevent, Suppress and Punish Trafficking in Persons, especially Women and Children, Supplementing the United Nations Convention against Transnational Organised Crime (Palermo Protocol). [51]

The rapid rate of ratification of these instruments, adding to international legal protection in this area, can be welcomed, although they have not yet attained the levels of ratification of Convention No.182.[52]

The ILO took an important initiative to curb the violation of *Child Rights* i.e. International Programme on the Elimination of Child Labour (IPEC) in 1992. India was among the first countries to participate in the programme. ILO-IPEC goes beyond trying to promote development by providing adequate educational alternative for children and access to decent work, sufficient income and security for their parents. The programme pays special attention to priority target groups, including the

---

[50] Adopted by General Assembly Resolution A/RES/54/263 of 25 May, 2000 and entered into force on 18th January, 2002.
[51] <http://www.ilo.org/public/english/standard/relin/itc/ilc95/pdf/rep-i-b.pdf>p.15 accessed on 15th June, 2013.
[52] *Ibid.*

girl child hidden work situations such as in sex trade and domestic services and other intolerable form of child labour. In India, the IPEC programme has been responding to national partners. Since its inception in 1992, as many as 154 projects have been implemented. These include rehabilitation of about 10,000/- child labour in different industries and sectors across the country, awareness rising capacity building and research[53]. The programme has also been working with voluntary organization and other civil societies group and institutions. IPEC has been working with the Employees Organization such as Council of Indian Employees and PUCCI as also with autonomous institution, like Central Board of Workers Education, National Labour Institute and the Maharashtra Institute of Labour Studies, to help them to eliminate child labour.

IPEC is now focusing on projects in certain areas of high concentration of child labour. Under an integrated area specific approach to be implemented through the National Child Labour Projects (NCLPs) run by the Government in different states. The ILO believes that the progressive elimination of child labour is possible through a change in attitudes on child labour. Poverty is no doubt major cause of child labour but education should be used as an instrument for reducing poverty through human capital development and skills. A unique initiative has been taken by ILO-IPEC by implementing an action programme with the help of Ruchika School Social Service Society, Bhubneshwar for the children who works on the platforms of Railway Stations.[54]

The UN System is committed to reduce and eventually eliminate child labour in India. For this the UN-Inter-Agency Working Group on Child Labour (IA WG-CL) was formed in September, 1998 which comprises of UNDP, ILO, UNESCO, WFP, UNIFEM and WHO. It is chaired and convened by ILO.

---

[53] UN News letter, 26th August, 2000.
[54] *Ibid.*

Keeping in view the strategies outlined in the UN position paper on child labour, the IA WG-CL proposes to take following activities ahead:

- Identify areas for collaboration between the UN agencies in current and planned programmes that have bearing on child labour with special focus on the girl child and children in hazardous occupations.
- Prepare a booklet on the work already being done by the various UN agencies that have an impact on child labour.
- Prepare a map indicating areas of work on UN agencies on child labour.
- Launch UN IAWG-CL Home Page.
- Sensitize the staff in UN agencies in the country on the child labour issues.
- Media advocacy and awareness raising on the ILO Convention No.182 on the worst forms of child labour, prioritize UN's work to eliminate worst form of child labour.
- Disseminate information and generate public awareness on child labour, particularly on the days like UN Day (October 24th), Children's Day (November 14th), November 19th (Day of coming into force of ILO Convention N:o.182) and November 20th (UN CRC Day)[55].

However, the harsh reality is that in India, ratification of International Labour Standards has been effective more as a 'status symbol' and for upholding the country's image abroad rather than for sincere implementation and compliance in practice. The ratification of UN Convention on the Rights of the Child by the Government of India is merely "a window dressing", says Swami Agnivesh,'[56] a social reformist, whereas the Constitution provides that state shall endeavor to foster respect for international law and treaty obligation in dealing with organized people, with one another.[57] The apex Court in cases such as *Mayan Bhai Ishwarlal Patel v.*

---

[55] *Ibid.*
[56] Main Stream 2nd Oct. 1983.
[57] Article 51(c), the Constitution of India, 1950.

Union of India[58] and *Vishaka v. State of Rajasthan*[59] has re-iterated the principle that in the absence of domestic law the contents of international convention and covenants are relevant for the purpose of interpretation of fundamental rights.

---

[58] AIR 1969 SC 783.
[59] (1997) 6 SCC 241.

CHAPTER III
CONCEPTUAL FRAMEWORK OF CHILD RIGHTS

In earlier times, children used to work within the family circle. Little by little, through almost imitation, they learnt the role they would be called upon to play as adults. During this process of socialization, of which his "on-the job" training formed a part, the child grew without ill-treatment and virtually without being exploited, and was simultaneously prepared for adult to work.[1] There was a widespread belief that children need useful and profitable work in order to make a natural and constructive entrance into the mainstream of the life of a community. An order of the "Great and General Courts of Massachusetts" in 1640 stated the obligation of parents and adult caretakers as follows:[2]

> *It is desired and will be expected that masters of families should see that their children and servants should be industriously employed so as the mornings and evenings and other seasons may not be lost or formerly they have been.*

This official expression represented a serious attempt to prevent idleness among children. It was considered to be a public duty to provide the training to children, not only with the purpose that children might learn but they might learn particular kinds of work, which would be profitable to the town and colonies. Alexander Hamilton, in 1791, urged that the new industry of spinning cotton performed by means of machine, which all put in motion by water and attended, chiefly by women and children, be encouraged. He noted that this industry had a dual advantage of serving as a means to contribute to general stock of industry and production and also giving employment to persons who would otherwise be idle and in many cases a burden on the society.[3]

---

[1] Elias Mendelievich Ed., *Children at work*,(ILO Publication, 1979), p.3.
[2] Edith Abbot, *Women in Industry: A Study in America Economic History,* (New York: Appleton, 1910), p. 328.
[3] Alexander Hamilton on the employment of children: American State Paper, Documents, Legislative and Executive of the congress of the United States from the first session to the first to third session of the Thirteenth Congress, Inclusive (Washington: 1832) Class-III, France", Vol.1,pp. 276-277.

As the industry expanded and became mechanized in the nineteenth century, a large number of children were employed in spinning and carding in textile mills. Children were made to work for long hours of ten-fourteen to sixteen hours a day. There were almost nil measures adopted in the name of safety and accidents were common. Corporal punishment was frequently used if children were lax at their work, as this laxity was frequently because of their immaturity, fatigue and poor health.

The movement of *Child Rights* is integrated with the movement to educate society that came with the Protestant Reformation view that everyone ought to be able to read Bible. Protestant churches and parishioners took over the responsibility of teaching children to read and write. Parents were permitted to use labour of their children in lieu of sending them to school. Gradually, the demand grew with regard to spending childhood time in training and development rather than work in mine mills and factories. The health hazard of children, which resulted from premature employment, was frequently cited as an argument in favour of child labour legislation. But the most persuasive argument by child reformers was that education was necessary in democracy. The battle within the states for compulsory school attendance for all children became a potent force in companion movement for legislation to protect children.

Unlike the western world, the rights of children were recognized in ancient India. In Vedic times, the life of man was divided into four ashrams i.e. Brahmcharya, Grastha, Vanprastha & Sanyasa. The age of a man was taken for 100 years and for each ashram 25 years were given. In Brahmcharya ashram, a child was sent to Gurukuls away from family for education. During this period, the child learned the basic morals and values followed in that society. Later on, this right to education remained confined to higher castes children only. But the position of children became bad to worse as the child slavery became a part of our society.

The rights of children have evolved over the years within the international community and all developments related to this issue had been codified in universal documents. The landmark in this relation was, the Convention on the Rights of the Child, which was unanimously adopted by the General Assembly of the United Nations[4] on 20th November, 1959. Article 1 of CRC[5] provides:

> For the purpose of the present Convention, a child means every human being below the age of 18 years unless under the law applicable to the child, majority is attained earlier.

The Article thus accommodates the concept of an advancement of majority at an earlier age either according to the federal or States Law of a country, or personal laws within that country. However, the upper limit on childhood is specified as an age of 'childhood' rather than majority, recognizing that in most legal systems, a child can acquire full legal capacity with regard to various matters at different ages.[6]

The Protocol to Prevent Suppress and punish Trafficking in Persons, especially Women and children, supplementing the United Nations Convention against Transnational Organized Crime,[7] Protocol to the Convention on the Rights of the Child on the involvement of children in armed conflict[8] and even the Convention concerning the Prohibition and Immediate Action for the Elimination of the Worst Forms of Child Labour, 1999[9] provides that child means any person below the age of 18 years. But the ILO Convention No. 138 on the minimum age for admission to employment and work lays down the following table concerning the minimum age of admission to employment and work.

	The minimum age at which children can start work.	Possible exceptions for developing countries

---

[4] United Nations Organization is an international Organization formed in 1944, which have pledged for maintenance of international peace and security.
[5] Convention on the Rights of the Child, 1989.
[6] Savities Goonesekar's *Children, Law and Justice: A South Asian Perspective*, (SAGE, 1998), p. 141.
[7] Article 3(d) "Child" shall mean any person under eighteen years of age.
[8] Article 1 States Parties shall take all feasible measures to ensure that members of their armed forces who have not attained the age of 18 years do not take a direct part in hostilities
[9] Article 2 For the purposes of this Convention, the term *child* shall apply to all persons under the age of 18.

Hazardous **work** Any work which is likely to jeopardize children's physical, mental or moral heath, safety or morals should not be done by anyone under the age of 18.	**18** **(16 under strict conditions)**	**18** **(16 under strict conditions)**
Basic **Minimum** **Age** The minimum age for work should not be below the age for finishing compulsory schooling, which is generally 15.	**15**	**14**
Light **work** Children between the ages of 13 and 15 years old may do light work, as long as it does not threaten their health and safety, or hinder their education or vocational orientation and training.	**13-15**	**12-14**

ILO[10] has the only conventions which acknowledge the child admission to employment below the age of 18 years. But rest all the convention at international level following the principle age limit laid down in Convention on Child Rights i.e. 18 years.

Accordingly, Indian legislation has minimum ages defined under various laws related to the protection of *Child Rights*.[11] Though legislation has been enacted to make 18 years the general age of majority in India, 21 years continues to be the upper limit for childhood for some purposes, partly due to the influence of nineteenth-century English Law and partly due to current exigencies.[12] For example, India recognizes 21 years as the age of majority in circumstances where a guardian has

---

[10] The ILO is the international organization responsible for drawing up and overseeing international labour standards. It is the only 'tripartite' United Nations agency that brings together representatives of governments, employers and workers to jointly shape policies and programmes.

[11] Implementation Hand Book for the Convention on the Rights of the Child, UNICEF, p. 1.

[12] *Child and Law*, Indian Council for Child Welfare, Chennai, Tamil Nadu, India, 1998, p. 210.

been appointed by the Court for a child below the age of 18 years[13] with respect to the rights of the child in the womb, the legislation in India is in harmony with the interpretation of the Convention. Significantly, Section 20 of the Indian Succession Act gives the right to property to a child in the womb whose parent's dies intestate and who is subsequently born alive-he/she will have the same right to inherit as if he or she had been born before the death of the parent.[14] The articulation of the 'right to life' in the Indian Constitution reflects the English Common Law approach, in that it states that this right is conferred on a "person". Although India has permitted medical termination of pregnancy through legislation enacted in 1971, this recourse can be taken only in the following cases (i) the continuance of pregnancy would involve a risk to the life of the Pregnant women or a grave injury to her physical and mental health or (ii) there is substantial risk that if the child born, it would suffer from such physical or mental abnormalities that it would be seriously handicapped.[15]

Varying ages of legal capacity is a phenomenon that can be seen in many countries. However, while the CRC's definition of childhood can be perceived as setting a basic minimum standard in view of Article 41,[16] which declares that "nothing in the convention or any of its provision shall effect any provision realization of the rights of the child" under the law of a state party, it is essential that there is some synchronization of the upper age limit for childhood.[17] India has achieved this to a large extent, for instance, the minimum compulsory age of education is 14 years. The various law relating to labour prohibit a person under the age of 14 years at work. Thus, the minimum age at which compulsory education ends

---

[13] *Ibid.*

[14] *Ibid.*

[15] Convention on the Rights of the Child: India First periodic Report- 2001 available at http://www.wcd.nic.in/crc.htm accessed on 15th September, 2013.

[16] Article 41 CRC provides: Nothing in the present convention shall affect any provision which are more conducive to the realization of the rights of the child and which may be contained in:

a)   The Law of a State Party; or

b)   International Law in force for the State.

[17] See *Supra* note 15.

synchronizes with the minimum age of employment.[18] The age of capacity to contract a marriage is 18 years for a girl and 21 years for a boy, for all communities. The Child Marriage Restraint Act, 1929, defines a child as a person who if a male, has not completed 21 years of age, and if a female has not completed 18 years of age. Under Section 5 of this Act whoever performs, conducts or directs any child marriage shall be punishable with simple imprisonment up to three months and shall also be liable to fine, unless he proves that he had reason to believe that the marriage was not a child marriage.[19] This uniform legislation is an effort to discourage child marriages under personal laws.[20]

It is evident that legislation is one of the main weapons of empowerment of children. Even though appropriate legislation may not necessarily mean that the objectives of the legislation will be achieved, its every existence creates an enabling provision whereby the State can be compelled to take action. Legislation reflects the commitment of the state to promote an ideal and progressive value system.[21] The different legislation has defined 'child' in different forms. The minimum legal age defined by national legislations is:[22]

	Age (Years)	
	Boys	Girls
Maximum age for compulsory education [23]	14	14

---

[18] No.NI/PC/SAP/132/2000/908, dated July 31, 2000, National Institute for Public Cooperation and Child Development, GOI, p. 4.
[19] See *Supra* note 12.
[20] *Ibid.*
[21] Asha Bajpai, *Child Rights in India: Law, Policy and Practice,* (Oxford University Press, New Delhi 2003), p. 6.
[22] See *Supra* note 15.
[23] Article 21(A), The Constitution of India, 1950 inserted by The Constitution (Eighty-Sixth Amendment) Act, 2002.

Marriage	21	18
Sexual consent	Not defined	16 if not married and 15 if married (Section 375 of the Indian Penal Code)
Voluntary enlistment in the armed forces	A person is allowed to take part in active combat only at the age of 18	
Conscription into the armed forces.	There is no conscription in India.	There is no conscription in India.
Participation in hostilities.	Not applicable.	Not applicable.
Admission to employment or work including hazardous work, part-time and full-time work.		
Child Labour (Prohibition and Regulation) Act, 1986.	14	14
Mines Act, 1952.	18	18
Merchant Shipping Act, 1958.	14	14
Motor Transport Workers Act, 1961.	14	14
Apprentices Act, 1961.	14	14
Beedi and Cigar Workers Act, 1966.	14	14
Factories Act, 1948[24]	14	14
Criminal responsibility	12	
	(Section 83 of the Indian Penal Code, according to which, nothing is an offence which is done by a child above seven years of age and under 12 years, who has not	

[24] An adolescent between fifteen and eighteen years can be employed in a factory only if he obtains a certificate of fitness from an authorized medical doctor.

	attained sufficient maturity of understanding to judge the nature and consequences of his conduct on that occasion. It may be noted that children below the age of seven years are deemed to be incapable of criminal offence as per section 82 of the Indian Penal Code)
Juvenile crime	18
	(The Juvenile Justice and Protection of Children) Act, 2000.
Deprivation of liberty, including by arrest, detention and imprisonment, inter-alia in the areas of administration of justice, asylum-seeking and placement of children in welfare and health institutions.	There is no age limit for deprivation of liberty because as per Article 21 of the Constitution of India, all citizens have protection to life and personal liberty which can be restricted only by following procedure established by law.
Capacity of contract[25]	18 Years
Capital punishment and life imprisonment.	18 Years
Giving testimony in court, in civil and criminal cases.	Section 118 of the Indian Evidence Act states that all persons shall be competent to testify unless the court considers that they are prevented from understanding the question put to them or from giving rational answers to those questions by tender years, extreme old age, disease, whether of body or mind, or any other cause of the same kind.

---

[25] Section 11, Indian Contract Act, 1872.

Lodging complaints and seeking redress before a court or other relevant authority without parental consent.	There is no minimum age prescribed for lodging complaints and seeking grievance before a court or other relevant authority without parental responsibility.	
Giving consent to change identity including change of name, modification adoption, guardianship.	18 For modification of family relations, adoption and guardianship, there is no minimum age prescribed.	
Having access to information concerning the biological family.	Not defined.	Not defined.
Legal capacity to inherit.	According to Section 20 of the Hindu Succession Act, even a child in the womb has the right to inherit property and it shall be deemed to from the date of death of one who died intestate. However, as per Section 4 of the Hindu Minority and Guardianship Act, 1956, the guardian will have the powers to take care of the property of such a minor.	
To conduct property transaction.	18	
To create or join association.	Not defined	Not defined.
Choosing a religion or attending religious school teachings.	Not defined.	Not defined.

In addition to above statutory rights, the Constitution of India also provides right to children, which includes fundamental rights and also Directive Principles of

State Policy. Some of the rights are included inclusively to ensure best interests of the child.

- Article 14 provides that state shall not deny to any person equality before law or equal protection of the law within the territory of India.
- Article 15 prohibits discrimination of citizens on the grounds only of religion, race, caste, sex, and place of birth or any of them.[26] But Article 15(3) provides that nothing in this Article shall prevent the State from making any special provision for women and children.
- Article 19 provides right to freedom including the freedom of speech and expression.[27]
- Article 21 provides no person shall be deprived of his life or personal liberty except according to procedure established by law.
- Article 21 A provides that the State shall provide free and compulsory education to all children of the age of six to fourteen years in such manner as the state may by law determine.[28]
- Article 23 prohibits "traffic in human beings", begar and forced labour.
- Article 24 prohibits employment of children in factories, etc.
- Article 25 to 28 provides freedom of conscience and profession, practice and propagation of religion.
- Article 39 (e) directs the state to ensure that the health strength of workers, men and women and the tender age of children are not abused.
- Article 39(f) directs the states to ensure that children are given opportunity and facilities to develop in a healthy manner and in conditions of freedom and

---

[26] Article 15 of the Constitution of India secures the right against discrimination, only to citizens and for that non-citizens cannot invoke the provisions of this Article.

[27] Article 19 of the Constitution of India guarantees to every citizen which include freedom of Speech and Expression; Freedom to assemble peacefully and without arms; freedom to form association or unions; freedom to reside and settle in any part of the territory of India; and freedom to practice and profession, or to carry on any occupation, trade or business.

[28] Inserted by The Constitution (Eighty-Sixth Amendment) Act, 2002.

dignity and that children and youth are protected against exploitation and against moral and material abandonment.

- Article 45 provides that the state shall endeavor to provide early childhood care and education for all children until they complete the age of six years.[29]
- Article 51 (k) lays down a duty that the parents or guardians should provide opportunities for education to his child/ward between the age of six and fourteen years.[30]

There does not appear to be any criteria or scientific parameter. For instance, in some laws as in Child Marriage Restraint Act 1929, there is a difference between the age of the boy and that of the girl. The minimum age of marriage for girls is eighteen but the age of sexual consent under the rape laws is sixteen and it is fifteen if she is married. The Mines Act defines children as those below eighteen years and the various state Shops & Establishment Acts define the age between twelve and fifteen years.[31] It is necessary that the definition of 'Child' be brought in conformity with the Convention on the Rights of Child, viz., below eighteen years of age. Though one may like to have a uniform age limit legally prescribed for the status of childhood, it may be perhaps not be possible or even desirable. Nevertheless, some rationalization is possible or some norms can be laid down as some of the age limits in the laws appear to be arbitrary or based on socio-cultural perceptions. The question of review of definition of 'Child' in the light of Article 1 of the Convention on the Rights of the Child has been referred to the Law Commission of India for consideration while undertaking a comprehensive review of the Code of Criminal Procedure, the Indian Evidence Act, and the Indian Penal Code.[32] There are more than 250 Central and State Statutes under which the child is covered in India.[33]

---

[29] *Ibid.*
[30] *Ibid.*
[31] See *Supra* note 21, p. 5.
[32] *Ibid.*
[33] State List i.e. List-II Entry 4: include prisons, reformatories, borstal institutions and other institutions of a like nature and persons detained therein; arrangements with other states for the use of prison and other institutions. The Concurrent list i.e. List-III Entry 5: Marriage and divorce, infants and minors, adoptions, wills, intestacy and succession, joint family and partition, all matters in respect of which parties in judicial

The principle of upholding the best interests of the child is not only reflected in the Constitution of India but also in the National Policy for children, the National Plan of Action for Children, the proposed National Charter for children and terms of reference of the proposed National Commission for children, as well as in other schemes and programmes related to children.[34] The best interest's principle is reflected in national legislation, Policies and Programmes laid down by the Government from time to time. But the struggle for the realization of the rights is indeed to be a long journey.

---

proceedings were immediately before the Commencement of the Constitution subject to their personal law. Entry 30 Vital Statistics including registration of birth and deaths Entry 41: Custody, management and disposal of property (including agricultural land) declared by law to be evacuee property.
[34] See *Supra* note 8, p. 6, 11-15.

CHAPTER IV
CHILD LABOUR IN INDIA

All adults stand accused......... The Society responsible for the welfare of children has been put on trial. There is something apocalyptic about this startling accusation; it is mysterious and terrible like the voice of the last judgment: "What have you done to the children that I entrusted to you?"

Maria Montessori

(The Secret of Childhood)

India's population is a pyramid of young person with children constituting large chunk. However, thousands of them die almost every day from causes as wide and varied as malnutrition, disease and neglect. It is quite disheartening to note that almost 50 percent of the total deaths in the country occur among children below five years. India had signed the *Convention on the Rights of the Child* on 11th December 1992 and ratified the Convention on January 1993. Some of the provisions[35] of the Constitution of India along with some decided cases[36] deal with the rights of Child. But still there are certain issues relating to children which need an immediate action. Some of the major violations of *Child Rights* present in our society have been discussed below:

4.1   Child Labour

Child labour has been defined as that "segment of child population which participates in work either paid or unpaid."[37] It generally concentrates on two concepts i.e. child in terms of chronological age and labour in terms of its nature,

---

[35] *Articles* 14, 15(3), 21, 23, 24, 39(f), 42, 45, 46, 47, The Constitution of India, 1950.
[36] PUDR v. U.O.I. AIR 1982 SC 1473; Laxmikant Pandey v. Union of India AIR 1984 SC 469; Sheela Barse v. Union of India AIR 1986 SC 1883; Unni Krishan, J.P. v. State of Andhra Pradesh (1993) (1) SCC 645; M.C. Mehta v. State of Tamil Nadu (1996) (6) SCC 756; Centre of Enquiry into Health and Allied Themes (CEHAT) & others v. Union of India & others AIR 2003 SC 301.
[37] Government of India, *Encyclopedia of Social Work in India I,* (1987), p.7.

quantum and income generation capacity.[38] Child labour is also explained as employment of children in gainful occupations or a material contribution to income of the family.[39] Again it means the employment of children under the specified legal age.[40] The term has been defined by U.S. Department of Labour as "the employment of boys and girls when they are too young to work for hire or when they are employed for jobs unsuitable or unsafe for children of their ages and under conditions injurious to their welfare."[41]

According to International Labour Organization (ILO), Child Labour is estimated at about 250 million worldwide. These children ranges between the age of 5 and 14 with around half of them working full time, of this figure, 140 million are boys and 110 million are girls. Sixty-one percent of them are located in Asia, 32 percent in Africa, and 7 percent in Latin America.[42] The problem of child labour exists all over the world in one form or another. But in this era of globalization, India is the major country of the world to employ child labour.

4.2. **Forms of Child Labour**

The evil of Child Labour in India has been in existence from the time immemorial. Though there was, little evidence of employment of children for wages, but if child slavery was accepted the existence of child labour in ancient India, cannot be denied. Slaves of tender ages, often less than eight years of age, were owned for doing low and ignorable work. Children of slaves were born as slaves, lived as slaves and died also as slaves unless the master was pleased to monument them. It has been noticed that almost all the law given with the solitary exception of Kautilya were silent on this point and did little to abolish this inhuman practice of keeping child slaves.[43] India in its medieval period was no exception. Increasing pressure on land led to fragmentation of holdings. Growing families had to look beyond personal

---

[38] *Ibid.*
[39] J.C. Kulshrestha, *Child Labour in India* (Asia Publishing House, New Delhi, 1978).
[40] New Encyclopedia Britannica Micropedia II, (15th ed. 1978), p.329.
[41] Encyclopedia Americana, (1963), p.461.
[42] Dolly Singh Ed., *Child Rights and Social Wrongs*, Volume 2, (Kanishka Publishers, Distributors, New Delhi, 2001), p.6.
[43] See *Supra* note 5, p.48.

cultivation for subsistence. A class of landless labourers came into existence, often bonded to the large land owners.[44] In brief, child labour in medieval India remained in existence on a large scale and even the rulers encouraged it with an intention to make only traffic in child slaves. The child labour was found in the form of child slavery and rulers did not endeavour to weed out this practice and hence, the result was that child was always exploited for this selfish ends. With the industrialization, the exploitation of children got increased. They had to work from morning till night for a pitiful earning. Near the middle of 19th century, the employers were free to bargain with labour with the result that children were employed in cotton, jute mills and coal mines etc. and were made to work mercilessly despite their tender age and were virtually converted into slaves. The Indian context is not confined to human rights alone, but incorporates dimensions that go beyond this realm, even transcend it. These include the following.[45]

- *The Historical Dimension:* Child Labour goes long back, it has a distinct and enduring rationale.

- *The Cultural Dimensions*: Child Labour is entwined in India's caste system and the acceptance of inequality associated with this form of social and economic stratification.

- *The Developmental Dimensions:* Child Labour relates to the structure of India's economy.

The major forms of child labour are listed below:[46]

- The first such kind is that of **domestic work**[47] e.g. cleaning, cooking, child care and other chores in the households in almost all type of societies.

---

[44] Manju Gupta, *"Child Labour: A Harsh Reality"*, *Child Labour in India,* (1987), p.2.
[45] <http://www.une.edu.acparts/SouthAsiaNet/ChildLabour/Child%20labour%20India.pdf.> accessed on 15th January, 2012.
[46] Employment News Weekly 9-15 October, 1999.
[47] Recently the Labour Ministry has issued a notification for imposing a ban on employment of children as domestic help or servants at road side kiosks which will come into effect from October 10, 2006.

- Another major form of child activities is in subsistence activities which are **non-domestic but non-monetary**. In agrarian economies, children are engaged in farms fuel and water collection.
- Another activity is **bonded labour.** This is the most exploitative form of child labour.
- Then comes **wage employment** where children are in employment either as part of a family group or individually in agricultural work sites, domestic services, manufacturing services.
- Child labour is also involved in **marginal work** e.g. work of short term or irregular nature like selling news papers, shoe shining, looking after cars, garbage collection and sorting out objects out of garbage.
- Another category comprises those children which lack access to school or are dropouts from the school. Such children having no employment wander into idleness and sometimes engage in anti-social activities. These are the children who engaged themselves in theft, prostitution and other socially undesirable activities. Practically, there is no industry in which children do not work directly or indirectly.

There are widely varying perception about the definition and concept of child labour and are three divided schools of thought, which are summed up as below:[48]

1.   The first school of thought treats education as the fundamental human right of every child in 5-14 age group and holds that any child in this age group who is out of school should be treated as a working child. According to this school, it is the responsibility of the State to create the infrastructure for facilitating free, compulsory and universal access to both primary and elementary education. They believe that there can be no excuse for over 100 million children in the 5-14 age group being outside the school system, whether formal and non-formal. They are firstly of the view that access to educational opportunity for all children in the 5-14 age group is

---

[48] Lakshmidhar Mishra, *Child Labour in India*, (Oxford University Press, New Delhi, 2000), pp.18-21.

the barest minimum obligation of the State and that the State cannot absolve itself from the obligation either on the ground of poverty and other economic compulsions or due to lack of infrastructure, logistical support and resource. They are also firmly of the view that it is child labour that induces poverty rather than poverty induces child labour. According to them, a child below 15 years of age is not physically and emotionally matures and fit to enter the world of work. If children is the 5-14 age group are being forced to work rather than being sent to school on account of social, economic and cultural compulsions such a process is bound to result in retardation and impoverishment of their evolution and growth to such an extent that when they cross the threshold of childhood, they will be too bereft of physical strength and energy to be productive and responsive adult members of society.[49]

According to them, all children of school-going age who are out of school should be presumed to be doing some form of work or the other. It is immaterial whether or not the job is hazardous as the concept of childhood does not fit into the world of work. They are, therefore, of the opinion that the distinction between hazardous and non-hazardous is at best artificial, and we cannot put up with a situation in which million of children are out of school spending their days at home or doing some work at home without wages or outside home for wages.[50]

2.   For the second school of thought, the magnitude of the problem is so enormous that the State will find it extremely difficult to create environment and provide the infrastructure, logistical support and resources to send the additional 100 million plus children to school. This school of thought, therefore, advocates a gradual, sequential and selective approach to the entire issue of out of school children viz-a-viz working children. Its supporters hold the view that we should first concentrate on those employed in hazardous occupation/process release and rehabilitate them through education, nutrition and skills training, and subsequently focus on those children who

---

[49] *Ibid.*
[50] *Ibid.*

are working in non-hazardous occupation/industries/processes. They believe that the elimination of child labour should be viewed as a long term goal to be achieved progressively rather than at a stroke. Since the total elimination of child labour by law is not possible therefore, they advocate a dual approach of prohibition and regulation, which is in sharp contrast with the view point of first school of thought supporting total prohibition.[51]

3.   There is third school of thought that maintains that both civil society and the State as the agent of the society has abjectly failed in (a) making education a fundamental human right (b) creating the appropriate infrastructure and environment and providing incentives to ensure access to educational opportunities to all, and (c) creating a positive and conducive environment that will enable universal retention and participation of children who have enrolled themselves in school and also make it possible for them to achieve at least the minimum levels of learning. They, therefore, recommend a point of view that militates against that of both the other schools of thought, in holding that it should be left to the children themselves to decide whether or not they want to go to school. If they want free universal elementary education, the necessary infrastructure, logistical support and environment for this should be created by the State on behalf of civil society. If, however, the children find that the educational system is dull, demotivating and irrelevant and would prefer to work, the state on behalf of the civil society should create opportunities for all forms of work that is in consonance with their physical and mental capacities.[52]

Each of the three schools of thought has its merits and demerits. The fact however, remains that every child is also a human being and human beings are the first products of creation. Childhood as a stage in the evolution and growth in human life is most tender, formative and impressionable.

---

[51] *Ibid.*
[52] *Ibid.*

4.3   Causes and Consequences of Child Labour

The phenomenon of working children is invariably associated with poverty and is usually considered to be a by-product of under-development. The highest incidence of child labour is said to be in the poorest countries of the world, and in the poorest regions of those countries. Globalization, indebtedness, and the widening income gap between the rich and poor countries may also exacerbate the problem. Several studies have pointed out that globalization does have a negative influence in the short term. Structural policies of adjustments have resulted in many developing countries spending less on basic services such as education. However, a crucial distinction has to be made between child labour and child work. Child work should be used as the generic term and should refer to any type of work in any mode of employment relationship. The concept of work, which is a description of a physical, mental involvement in a job, may be an activity, which, rather than being harmful, is beneficial to the child in its formative socialization. The concept of labour, on the other hand, should be restricted to the production and services which interfere with the normal development of children as defined by the CRC.[53]

There is a perception that quite a lot of what has been subsumed under child labour, is actually work performed during a standard process of socialization and not associated with labour exploitation or interfering with the quality of development which the child in the given circumstances could except.[54] The cases that lead to child labour are:[55]

- Poverty.
- Parental illiteracy and ignorance.
- Traditions of making children learn the family skills.
- Absence of universal compulsory primary education.

---

[53] Convention on the Rights of the Child: India First periodic Report- 2001 available at http://www.wcd.nic.in/crc.htm accessed on 15th September, 2013. .

[54] G.K. Lieten, *Children Work and Education I- General Parameters,* Economic and Political Weekly, June 10, 2000.

[55] Helen Sekar, *Ensuring their childhood,* V.V.Giri National Labour Institute, New Delhi, (2001).

- Non-availability of and non-accessibility to schools.
- Irrelevant and non-attractive school curriculum.
- Social and cultural environment.
- Informalization of production.
- Employer's preference of children for their cheap labour and inability to organize against exploitation.
- Family work.
- Level of technology.
- Apathy of Trade Unions.
- Ineffective enforcement of the legal provisions pertaining to child labour.

Child labour often creates a vicious circle of poverty, as a child coming from an impoverished family surviving harsh conditions become an unskilled, debilitated adult who is not employed even in the industry that exploited him/her earlier. Furthermore, child labour receives a low, negligible income and often no wages at all. They have no rights as workers and may not join trade union. Child labour also depresses adult labour and keeps adults unemployed.[56] Although a major cause, poverty alone does not cause child labour. As ILO rightly warns: [57]

> *"Poverty is not the only reason for the existence of child labour. The picture varies across households and across regions and countries. Countries which are equally poor may yet have relatively high or relatively low levels of non-school-going children or of working children. Underlying child labour obviously also is the full factor, the desire to maximize profits and to command an utmost docile and flexible labour force. The absence of a strong (adult) labour movement and a strong civic society in general, in combination with the interalia of government institutions will allow these tendencies a free hand."*
> *Thus, child labour is essentially associated with inequality in society.*

---

[56] Vikas Adhyayan Kandra, *facts Against Myths*, Vol.III, 8, 1996 p.2.
[57] <http://www.wcd.nic.in/crc.pdf/CRC-8-PDF> accessed on 10th January, 2012.

In India, the co-relation between child labour and regional poverty is inconclusive. Some of the richer States also have a higher child labour count. Literacy rate is another important variable which explain the differences in the ratios of child employment. Kerala furnishes a strong co-relation between literacy and the decline of child labour. It is not merely economic development but the overall social development including basic education which plays a major role in the decline of incidence of child labour. This is the reason why Kerala has a lower incidence of child labour than Punjab, Haryana and several other States which have lower poverty ratios. An important fact that has been established by many surveys is that access to education is a general wish among parents and children, but this remains unfulfilled due to the lack of proper functioning government schools.[58]

Consequences of Child Labour

Sending children to work may seems to a genuine approach to poverty stricken families but the employment has profound repercussions. ILO research shows that child labour is universally recognized as being undesirable, harmful for the children themselves. Mendelievich, in his book, has classified repercussions of child labour into three forms:[59]

a) ***Social and Labour Repercussions:***

When a child joins the work force at a young age, he is deprived of the opportunity to educate himself and acquiring qualifications which will help in getting a better job in future. It is, therefore, quite apparent that a child who has been at work from an early age will spend his whole life at the bottom of the social ladder. Thus, child labour has become a mode of perpetuating an unjust social system and of ensuring the continued availability of subservient unskilled, illiterate labourers who does not have the bargaining power to question the system that marginalizes them and deprives them of their right to lead a decent life.[60]

---

[58] See *Supra* note 20.
[59] Elias Mendelievich, *Children at Work*, (ILO Publication, 1979), p.46.
[60] *Ibid.*

b)   *Physical Repercussions:*

Many of the jobs that children do are harmful for their physical development. The physical susceptibility of working children also has a lot to do with the fact that they are different capacities and needs from adults and this fact is very rarely taken into account by employers. The manner, nature and conditions of their employment lead to serve health and safety hazards. In agriculture also there are certain hazards which have particularly increased due to the introduction of advanced farming practices, new techniques and chemicals. However, these problems are aggravated in industries where work is heavy and involve the use of sharp and dangerous objects and toxic substances. The risks of occupational diseases or accidents are higher among child workers because their growing bodies are not as strong as adult workers. The table below mentioned gives an overview of occupational hazards faced by working children.[61]

Occupational Hazards

Occupation	Related Diseases/Disabilities
Tile Industry	Tuberculosis, skin discolouration and allergic eruptions.
Slate Industry	Tuberculosis, silicosis, respiratory diseases.
Match Industry/Fireworks Industry.	Tuberculosis, respiratory diseases, skin diseases such as dermatitis, severe eye-strain, night blindness and premature blindness.
Powerloom Industry	Byssinosis, fibrosis, bronchitis and tuberculosis.
Glass Industry	Pneumoconiosis, tuberculosis, burns, life span reduced by a third due to intense heat and dust, and night blindness.

---

[61] See supra note 8, p.234.

Pottery Industry	Asthamatic bronchitis, tuberculosis, silicosis.
Brass Industry	Acid burns, tuberculosis and other respiratory tract problems.
Bidi Industry	Chronic bronchitis and tuberculosis.
Diamond Industry	Severe eye-strain, tuberculosis, and other lung diseases.
Carpet Weaving Industry	Tuberculosis and other lung diseases, eye-strain, night blindness.
Lock Industry	Tuberculosis and other respiratory tract diseases, asthma and acute headaches.
Balloon Industry	Pneumonia, broncho-pneumonia, cough, breathlessness and even heart failure.
Zari Industry	Eye diseases, spondylitis and lead poisoning.
Agarbatti Industry	Rheumatism of wrist elbows, breathing problems, skin and eye diseases.

Thus many jobs done by the children are the cause of physical deformities and illness such as deformities of spine, stunted growth, infections, burns, sores etc or else they may aggravate defects or maladies. Child labour involves both short-term and long-term health risks. Some of the hazards may not be immediately apparent but may take some years to manifest.

c) *Mental Repercussions:*

Child labour has mental repercussions also since the age at which child usually starts to work coincides more or less with a period of profound mental change in the child. Clearly, if to the working child's unfavourable intellectual status is added an ill-directed mental development there will be undesirable mental consequences and behavioral problems caused by the child's in adequate comprehension of the adult world and by his imitating, distorting and exaggerating what he wrongly believes to be essence of that world. The mental consequences of child labour are not just the result of the work situation but the violent change to which the child is exposed. Moreover, since a large number of children work for long hours, their social interactions are limited and this affects their emotional development. Lack of leisure time activities and repression of childhood desires have harmful impact on the harmonious development of a child personality.[62]

Keeping in account, all the adverse effect of child labour, India has all along followed a pro-active policy with respect to the problem of child labour. Six ILO Conventions relating to child labour have been ratified, three of these as early as the first quarter of the 20th century.[63] The framers of Indian Constitution consciously incorporated relevant provisions in the Constitution for the protection of children both in Fundamental Rights and Directive Principles of State Policy.[64] Despite the Constitutional, legislative, policy framework in India the problem of child labour still persists.

---

[62] See *Supra* note 25.

[63] India has signed following ILO Convention :

Convention No.5 of 1919 – provides that children under the age of 14 years should not be employed in industrial undertaking. Ratified by India on September 9, 1955.

Convention No.6 of 1919- provides that employment of children under 18 years of age during night hours in public or private industrial undertaking. Ratified by India on August 7, 1921;

Convention No.15 of 1921 – provides that young person under the age of 18 years are not to be employed on vessels as trimmers or stokers. Ratified by India on November 20, 1922;

Convention No.16 of 1921 – provides for compulsory medical examination of children and young persons employed at sea. Ratified by India on November 20, 1922.

Convention No.90 of 1948 – partly revises Convention No.6 of 1919. Ratified by India on February 27, 1950.

Convention No.123 of 1965 – provides that the minimum number of young persons to work in an underground mine, should be fixed in consultation with the employers and workers, organizations and that the age should not be less than 16 years. Ratified by India on March 20, 1975.

[64] *Article 24* of the Constitution of India – No Child below the age of 14 years shall be employed to work in any factory or mine or engaged in any other hazardous employment.

Article 39 of the Constitution of India - The State shall in particular, direct its policy towards securing.

that the health and strength of workers men and women and the tender age are not abused and the citizens are not forced by economic activity to enter a vocation unsuited to their age or strength.

That children are given opportunities and facilities to develop in a healthy manner and in condition of freedom and dignity and that childhood and youth are protected against exploitation and against moral and material abandonment.

CHAPTER V

RIGHTS OF THE CHILD UNDER INDIAN CONSTITUTION

Prohibition of child labour and provision for compulsory universal, primary education for all children up to the age of fourteen have been advocated long before Independence. In 1906, Gopal Krishna Gokhale, the then President of the Indian National Congress, unsuccessfully urged the British Government to establish free and compulsory elementary education. The movement continued. With the setting up of the Constituent Assembly in 1949, it was resolved that the future Constitution of India would provide for abolishing child labour and ensure compulsory education to children. The reference was made to Article 23 para 2 of the Yugoslavian Constitution in this regard which prohibits the employment of children in mines, factories or other hazardous jobs.[1] The matter was discussed in the Constituent Assembly with all concern. Significantly, the draft constitution prepared by the Drafting Committee contained provisions for prohibition of child labour and for free and compulsory education for children.

Article 18[2] of the Draft Constitution provided ban on the employment of children below 14 years of age in any factory or mine or engaged in any other hazardous employment. It reads as:[3]

No child below the age of 14 years shall be employed in any factory or mine or engaged in other hazardous activities.

Sh. Damodar Swarup Seth while expressing his views with regard to affording protection to children of minor age also suggested an addition to the said article for prohibiting employment of women workers at night in order to protect their health.[4]

---

[1] *The Framing of India's Constitution,* A study by B. Shiva Rao, (The Indian Institute of Public Administration, 1966), p.251 [See B.N. Rau's notes, select Document II, 4 (v) (c), p.149].
[2] Corresponding to Article 24 of the enacted Constitution.
[3] See *Supra* note 1.

Prof. Shibban Lal Saksena also advocated the amendment proposed by Sh. Damodar Swarup Seth. He said that he was very glad that this article has been placed among fundamental rights. Infact, one of the complaints against this charter of liberty is that it does not provide for sufficient economic rights. If we examine the fundamental rights in the Constitutions of other countries, we will find that many of them are concerned with economic rights. In Russia, particularly, the right to work alongwith, the right to rest and leisure, the right to maintenance in old age and sickness etc., are guaranteed. We have provided these rights in our Directive Principles, although it was thought, that they should be incorporated in this chapter. Even then, this article 18 is an economic right that no child below the age of fourteen shall be employed in any factory. He further suggested that the age should be raised to sixteen. In other countries, also the age is higher, and they also want that in our country this age should be increased particularly on account of our climate, children are weak at this age and the age should be raised.[5]

Article 36[6] in the Draft Constitution provided free and compulsory education to all children below 14 years of age. Pandit Lakshmi Kanta Maitra moved an amendment that in Article 36, the words *"Every citizen is entitled to free primary education"* be deleted. It was proposed that after amendment Article 36 would be read as follows.

That state shall endeavor to provide, within a period of ten years from the commencement of this Constitution, for free and compulsory education for all children until they complete the age of fourteen years.

The purpose for amendment was that the Article 36 is a Directive Principle of State policy but the words "Every citizen is entitled to ....etc" is not into line with

---

[4] Shri Damodar Swarup Seth moved an amendment in this article. He wanted to add the following at the end of *Article 18*: 'Nor shall women be employed at night, in mines or in industries detrimental to their health', *Constituent Assembly Debates*, Volume-VII, p.814.

[5] *Ibid.*

[6] Corresponding to *Article 45* of the enacted Constitution.

the preceding and subsequent articles. This article resembles Fundamental Rights in its wording. This cannot be fit with others directive principles of State policy. Another reason is that, the education should not be confined to the primary but it may go upto the secondary stage, so long as the person is up to the age of 14.[7]

Dr. B.R. Ambedkar accepted the proposed amendment that every child shall be kept in an educational institution under training until the child is of 14 years. Dr. B.R. Ambedkar supported this amendment with the view of Mr. Nazirruddin Ahmed who has given the objective behind this article and referred to Article 18, which forms part of the fundamental rights, it would have been noticed that a provision is made in Article 18 to forbid any child being employed below the age of 14 obviously, if the child is not to be employed below the age of 14, the child must be kept occupied in some educational institution that was object of Article 36, and that is why the word 'primary' is quite in appropriate in the particular clause.[8]

The Fundamental Rights enacted in Part-III operate as limitations on the powers of the State and impose negative obligations on the State not to encroach on individual liberty and they are enforceable not only against State. But there are certain Fundamental Rights conferred by the Constitution which are enforceable against the whole world and they are found inter-alia in Article 17, 23 and 24.[9] Article 23 was incorporated in the Constitution to prohibit traffic in human beings and begar and other similar forms of forced labour. The reason for enacting this provision in the chapter of Fundamental Rights is to be found in the socio-economic conditions of the people at the time of enactment of the Constitution.

The Constitution makers, when they set out to frame the Constitution, found that they had the enomorous task before them of changing the socio-economic structure of the country and bringing about socio-economic regeneration with a view

---

[7] See *Supra* note 4.
[8] See *Supra* note 4.
[9] P.U.D.R. v. Union of India AIR 1982, SC 1473, p.1485.

of reaching social and economic justice to the common man. Large masses of people, lived two centuries of white foreign rule, were living in abject poverty and destitution with ignorance and illiteracy accentuation their helplessness and despair. The society had degenerated into status-oriented hierarchical society with little respect for the dignity of the individual who was in the lower rungs of the social ladder or in an economically impoverishment condition. The political revolution was completed and it had succeeded in bringing freedom to the country but freedom was not an end, the end being the raising of the people to higher levels of achievement and bringing about their total advancement and welfare. Political freedom has no meaning unless it was accompanied by social and economic freedom and it was, therefore, necessary to carry forward the social and economic revolution with a view to create socio-economic conditions in which every one would be able to enjoy basic human rights and participate in the fruits of freedom and liberty in an egalitarian social and economic framework. It was with this end view, that the framers of the Constitution enacted the Directive Principles of State policy in Part-IV of the Constitution, setting out the constitutional goal of a new socio-economic order.[10]

Article 39(f) enjoins that the State shall direct its policy towards securing that children are given opportunities and facilities to develop in a healthy manner and in conditions of freedom and dignity and the childhood and youth are protected against exploitation and against moral and material abandonment.[11] This article was incorporated with the background that the economic system of our country at the time of independence was such that women might be forced by sheer necessity to take occupation which may not be suitable to the conditions imposed on them by nature. To avoid these complications the members of Drafting Committee has incorporated this Article.[12]

---

[10] *Ibid.*

[11] Article 31(v) of the Draft Constitution enjoined that the State shall direct its policy towards securing the health and strength of workers; men and women; and the children of tender age will not be abused; the citizens should not be forced to enter avocations unsuited to their age and strength. The Article 39 was discussed under Article 31 by the drafting Committee and later on it was renumbered.

[12] See *Supra* note 4.

Prof. Shibban Lal Saxsena also advocated a socialist system in our country. He said that we have here magnificent and sparkling words i.e. social justice, political justice and economic justice, which are very splendid words but they appear very far away from the toiling millions. Why not state here, not today, not tomorrow, but in the distant future that the community will owe, what belongs to the community by the gift of nature and, by gift of God. He also stated that though he did not belong to the Socialist party yet he appealed to Dr. B.R. Ambedkar who claims to represent the downtrodden untouchables of the country not to wash away this hope from their hearts that in the future years the natural resources of the community may belong not to the privileged few but to the poor people of the country, for the good and benefit of all.[13]

Although the Directive Principles are not enforceable or justifiable in this way, they were nevertheless viewed as being fundamental to the governance of the country. Their significance was lucidly and forcefully enunciated by Dr. B.R. Ambedkar in a statement made in the Constituent Assembly:[14]

In enacting this part of the Constitution, the Constituent Assembly is giving certain directions to the future legislatures and the future executives to show in what manner they are to exercise the legislative and the executive power they will have. Surely, it is not the intention to introduce in this part these principles as mere pious declarations. It is the intention of the Assembly that in future both the legislature and the executive should not merely pay lip service of these principles as mere pious declaration. Instead they should be the basis of all legislative and executive action that they may be taking hereafter in the matter of governance of the country.

The same spirit was reflected in yet another statement[15] by Pandit Jawahar Lal Nehru.

---

[13] *Ibid.*
[14] Lakshmidhar Mishra, *Child Labour in India,* (Oxford University Press, New Delhi, 2000), p.163.
[15] *Ibid.*

The service of India means the service of the millions who suffer. It means the ending of poverty and ignorance and disease and inequality of opportunity. The ambition of the greatest man of our generation has been to wipe every tear from every eye. That may be beyond us but as long as there are tears and suffering so long our work will not be over.

It is well-known that work, unless it is creative, interesting and challenging can be extremely harmful to the young children. That is not to undermine the dignity of manual labour, but merely to point out that there are strict limitations on the forms, content and extent of work that young children can safely undertake. How can children afflicted with malnutrition and other crippling disabilities be expected to cope up with stress and exhaustion of work and at the same time grapple with the rigors of non-formal education. It is necessary to ponder over the questions and what is likely to lead to before making a policy decision and implementing it. The legislature in its wisdom very aptly appreciated that mere release of the child labourers without making appropriate arrangements for his rehabilitation will serve no useful purpose and, may even create a very real problem as to livelihood of the labourers so set free and, accordingly the legislation made suitable provision for the rehabilitation of child labourers.

This was the first step of independent India to provide a social and economic freedom to all Indians. It is quite clear, that mere passing of welfare legislation for the upliftment of the down trodden, the meek and weak is by itself not sufficient, though undoubtedly the legislation is the first step in right direction and this step is taken by our constitution makers in 1948. But the real and most important thing which is required is that every law enacted, particularly welfare legislation for the benefit of the weaker section of the people, must be implemented in the proper spirit for achieving the noble object for which legislation is passed. Implementing, the law has, necessarily to be effected through human agencies. Unfortunately, frailties of human nature and degeneration of human character often add to existing problem, instead of solving them.[16]

The Constitution as was finally adopted on 29th November, 1949 contained provisions for the protection of children. The Constitution guarantees special protection to children. The relevant provisions in this regard are discussed below:

Article 15(3) provides that *"Nothing in this Article shall prevent the State from making any special provision for women and children"*. This clause is an exception to the rule against discrimination embodied in clause (1) as well as clause (2) of the above referred Article.[17] Clause (3) enables the State to confer special rights upon children. Thus, law regarding separate accommodation for children at places of public resort, restricting hours of labour for children is not prohibited. In the same way laws prohibiting employment of children below a particular age, employment of children in hazardous or injurious work are also saved. These laws are passed taking into consideration the physical structure of the child.

Article 24 provides that *"No child below the age of fourteen years shall be employed to work in any factory or mine or engaged in any other hazardous employment"*. It must be noted that this Article does not create an absolute ban to the employment of child labour. In the first place, this Article applies only to children below the age of 14 years. Secondly even in case of the children below 14 years, this Article only prohibits the employment of children in a factory or mine or in any other hazardous employment.

---

[16] *Ibid.*

[17] Article 15(1) provides: *"The State shall not discriminate against any citizen on grounds only of religion race, caste, sex, place of birth or any of them"*
Article 15(2) provides: *"No citizen shall, on grounds of religion, race, sex, place of birth or any of them, be subjected to any disability, liability, restriction or condition with regard to-*
a) *access of shops, public restaurants, hotels and places of public entertainments; or*
b) *the use of wells, tanks, bathing ghats, roads and places of public resort maintained wholly or partly out of State funds or dedicated to the use of general public."*

The Supreme Court has interpreted this clause to provide protection and security to the children. In the case of *labourers working on Salal Hydro Project v. State of Jammu and Kashmir,*[18] the apex Court said that the construction work was a hazardous employment and hence no child below the age of 14 years could be allowed to be employed in the construction work.

The child labourers are firstly children and then labourers. As such they should also not be treated cruelly and in humanly. In *Bandhua Mukti Morcha v. Union of India,*[19] Justice P.N. Bhagwati interpreted Articles 21 and 24 of the Constitution and held;

> *"It is the Fundamental right to every one in this country assured under the interpretation given to Article 21.... To live with human dignity..... **It must include the tender age of children against abuse, opportunities and facilities for children to develop in a health manner and in condition** of freedom and dignity, **educational relief.** These are the minimum requirements which must exist in order to enable a person to live with human dignity and neither the Central Government nor State Government has, the right to take any action which will deprive a person of the enjoyment of these basic essentials which go to make up a life of human dignity".*

However, it remains a bitter truth that in most of the cases the little workers are not provided adequate medical care, rehabilitation and educational facilities, good food service, payment of normal subsistence allowance and so on.

---

[18] AIR 1984 SC 177, Apex Court has also re-iterated the same principle in P.U.D.R. v. U.O.I. AIR 1982 SC 1473 that construction work is hazardous and State Government should take immediate steps for inclusion of construction in the schedule of Employment of Children Act, 1938.

[19] AIR 1984 SC 802, Bandhua Mukti Morcha, is an organization dedicated to the cause of release of bonded labourers, informed the Supreme Court through a letter that they have conducted a survey of the stone-quarries situated at Faridabad of the State of Haryana and found that there were a large number of labours working in these stone quarries under "inhuman and intolerable conditions." The Court treated a letter a writ petition, p.811.

The another step to prohibit child labour was taken in ***M.C. Mehta v. State of Tamil Nadu and others***[20] where Supreme Court in order to tackle the problem of child labour issued directions to the State Governments to fulfill the legislative intention behind the Constitutional provision. The Court while taking guidance from Child Labour (Prohibition and Regulation) Act, 1986 further directed that the offending employer must be asked to pay compensation for every child employed in contravention of the provisions of the Act a sum of Rs.20,000/- and the inspectors, whose appointment is visualized by Section 17 to secure compliance with the provision the Act, should do this job. The inspectors appointed under Section 17 would see that each child employed in violation of the provisions of the Act, the concerned employer pays Rs.20,000/- which sum could be deposited in a fund to be known as Child Labour Rehabilitation-cum-Welfare fund. The liability of the employer would not cease even if he would desire to disengage the child presently employed. It would perhaps be appropriate to have such a fund district wise or area wise. The fund so generated shall from corpus whose income shall be used only for the concerned child. The quantum could be the income earned on the corpus deposited qua the child. To generate greater income, fund can be deposited in high yielding scheme of any nationalized bank or other public body. In the end, the Hon'ble Ld. Judges of Supreme Court said that they part with the hope that the closing years of the twentieth century would see us keeping the promise made to our children by our constitution about a half-century ago.[21]

Further Article 45[22] expressed that "the *State shall endeavor to provide within a period of 10 years from the commencement of the Constitution free and compulsory education for all children until they complete the age of fourteen years.*"

---

[20] AIR 1997 SC 699.

[21] The copies of this judgment is to be sent to Chief Secretaries of all the State Governments and Union Territories so also to the Secretary, Ministry of Labour, Government of India for their information and doing the needful.

[22] Before the enforcement of the Constitution (Eighty-Sixth Amendment) Act, 2002.

This directive should have been implemented by the end of January 1960. But the State could not keep the time limit for its implementation, as during the year 1960-61 only 62.40% of the children of 6-11 age group and 22.5% of the 11-14 age group were going to a school.[23] Thus it is evident that time limit has not been considered by the State to be the essence of the mandate of Article 45. The total literacy rate in India in 2001 is 65.38 percent consisting of 75.85 percent men and 54.16 percent women.[24] There are, however, wide variations across regions, states, castes, classes and sexes. Realizing the delayed tactics the Supreme Court in **Unni Krishan v. State of Andhra Pradesh**[25] held that the right of education upto the age of 14 years is a fundamental right within the meaning of Article 21 of the Constitution. The rights to education flows directly from the right to life. It further stated that it is noteworthy that among the several Articles in Part-IV, only Article 45 speaks of time limit, no other Article does. Has it got some significance? Is it a mere pious wish, even after 44 years of the Constitution? Neera Burra, renowned social workers has also felt that if there is at all a blue print for tackling the problem of child labourer, it is education.[26]

The Constitution (Ninety Third Amendment) Bill, 2001 provided to make free and compulsory education to all citizens of the age group of 6-14 years, a fundamental right, by inserting Article 21A in the Constitution. Further, under Article 51 A of the Constitution, after clause (J) the following clause was suggested to be added namely clause (k) to provide opportunities for education to a child between the age of six and fourteen years of whom such citizen is a parent or guardian.[27]

---

[23] *Position of Child under Indian Constitution,* Chandra Pal paper presented in Seminar held in Panjab University on ,*Child and Law,* Ed. Paras Diwan,(1980), p. 461.
[24] UNICEF in India 1999-2002 – Challenges and Opportunities UNICEF.
[25] 1993(1) SC 645. The petitioner running Medical and Engineering Colleges in State of Andhra Pradesh, Karnataka, Maharastra and Tamil Nadu contented that if Mohini Jain decision is correct and followed by their respective State Government they will have to close down their colleges.
[26] See *Supra* note 20, p.709.
[27] The Constitution (Eighty-Sixth Amendment), Act, 2002.

- The amendment makes education as a fundamental right for children in the age group of 6-14 years.[28]
- The State shall endeavor to provide early childhood care and education for all children until they complete the age of six years.[29]
- It shall be the fundamental duty of the parents and guardians to provide opportunities for education to their children or, as the case may be, words between the age six and fourteen years.[30]

The Right of Children to Free and Compulsory Education Act, 2009 is the first central and most awaited legislation relating to education. The Act was notified by the central government on April 1, 2010. The Act aims at Free and Compulsory education for all children from six to fourteen years. The salient features of the Act are:

- Every child in the age group of 6-14 has the right to free and compulsory education in a neighborhood school, till the completion of elementary education
- Private schools will have to take 25% of their class strength from the weaker section and the disadvantaged group of the society through a random selection process. Government will fund education of these children.
- A child above six years of age has not been admitted in any school or though admitted, could not complete his or her elementary education, then, he or she shall be admitted in a class appropriate to his or her age; Provided that where a child is directly admitted in a class appropriate to his or her age, then, he or she shall, in order to be at par with others, have a right to receive special training, in such manner, and within such time limits, as may be prescribed: Provided

---

[28] A new Article has been inserted, namely: *Article 21A* provides: *"The State shall provide free and compulsory education to all children of the age of six to fourteen years in such a manner as the State may by law, determine."*

[29] *Article 45* has been substituted, Now *Article 45* provides: *"The State shall endeavor to provide early childhood care and education for all children until they complete the age of six years."*

[30] In *Article 51A* of the Constitution a new clause has been added, namely *Article 51 A(k)* *"who is parent or guardian to provide opportunities for education to his child or as the case may be, ward between the age of six and fourteen years".*

further that a child so admitted to elementary education shall be entitled to free education till completion of elementary education even after fourteen years.

- No school or person shall be allowed to take capitation. Parent, child or guardian shall not be subject to screening procedure. No child can be held back, expelled and required to pass the board examination till the completion of elementary education.

- Three years time period has been provided to school to implement all the norms and standards required under section 18 of the Act.

- All schools except private unaided schools are to be managed by School management Committees with 75% of parents and guardians as members

This is the first Central Legislation on primary education in Schools. It can be said to be a revolutionary step for the first time in our country to ensure education to children. But this Act is also not free from defects. Firstly, the Central Rules was notified on 9th April 2010, while as per the official release made at the end of the first year of the Act, as of 1st April 2011 only 9 out of 29 States (such as Andhra Pradesh, Arunachal Pradesh, Chhattisgarh, Haryana, Madhya Pradesh, Manipur, Orissa, Rajasthan and Sikkim) notified their Rules and only 2 out of 6 UTs (namely, Andaman & Nicobar Islands and Chandigarh) adopted the Central Rules. Thus, legally speaking the Act is non-existent in more than two thirds of India's States/UTs. Pre-school support is essential for children and ignoring the children below six years age group could lead to promotion of child labour.

The concept of neighbourhood schools is central to the Common School System. The Kothari Commission Report recommended that each school within the Common School System should be attended by all the children in the neighbourhood. The Act doesn't follow the idea of Common School System laid down. The education System which has been developed is increasing social segregation and perpetuating and widening class distinctions because many government schools are of poor quality while private schools are better off in many ways. Private Schools could only be afforded by middle and top class of the society. Professor Amartya Sen recently emphasised education as an important parameter for any inclusive growth in an economy. The policies have to focus on *inclusive rather than divisive growth strategies.* Corporate India moving towards this sector is laudable, but it is clear that deficiency in education cannot be met by mere expansion of private schools in urban areas. "Public education is as indispensable as public health care, no matter what supplementary role private schools and private medical care can play

CHAPTER VI

RIGHTS OF THE CHILD UNDER THE LABOUR LAWS

The dawn of Industrial Revolution in Europe witnessed, the growing awakening against the systematic exploitation of children, protective legislation for non-employment of children below a certain age and providing for a guaranteed minimum wage were the end products towards the fulfillment of this awakening. In India the gravity of the problem came to light with the various commissions and committees, which had been set up to look into various facets of labour problems. The earliest full scale exercise in this regard was the work done by Whitely Commission (Royal Commission on Labour), in 1931. Labour Investigation Committee (1944-46) also made useful contribution in this regard. Then in this chain is the Report of National Commission on Labour (1969) and the latest one in this regard was Report of Second National Labour Commission (2001).

Royal Commission on Labour in 1931 was a milestone in the area of the *Child Rights*. The Commission stated:[1]

> "....*In many cities large number of boys are employed for long hours and discipline is strict. Indeed, there is reason to believe that corporal punishment and other disciplinary measures of a reprehensible kind are sometimes resorted to in the case of smaller children. Workers as young as five years of age may be found in some of these places working without adequate meal intervals or weekly rest days, and 10 or 12 hours daily sums as low as 2 annas in case of those of tenderest years.*"

It accordingly recommended legislation to fix the minimum age of employment of children at a level higher than that prevailing in the industries. Another development in area of employment of child labour was reached with the appointment of labour Investigation Committee in 1944. Set up by the Government of

---

[1] Report of Royal Commission on Labour. (Calcutta: Government of India Central Publication Branch, 1931), pp.96-97.

India, the Committee was asked to investigate, interalia, questions relating to employment of children. It observed.[2]

> *"The important fact that has emerged from investigations is that in various industries, mainly smaller industries, the prohibition of employment of children is disregarded quite openly, and owing to the inadequacy of the inspection staff it has become difficult to enforce the relevant provisions of the law".*

The National Commission on labour (1969) found the poverty responsible for the employment of children at the cost of their education.[3]

> *"During the course of our observational visits, we found prevalence of child labour in handloom and power loom units usually a weaver has as it his mate a child of the school going age. The education of the mate is no concern of weaver nor of the person who engages the weaver. Children are not direct employees, but they help the weaver and collect whatever money they can get from him. In due course they learn the trade. If the education of a child is a casualty in the process it is the poverty of the parents which is to be blamed. Brocade work is another intricate operation where child labour is quite common. In the units we inspected, the proprietor assured us that though the boys who were working there looked between 8-10 years of age or even younger, they were all above 14, the age at which adolescents were permitted to be engaged under the local rules. In several cases, we were told, the payment to the child was the responsibility of the adult worker whom the child helped. When the former himself gets a low wage, he could be parting with but little of it for his helper. The whole arrangement appeared to be exploitative when seen in relation to the fact such operations were carried on so near the factory premises. A similar arrangement prevails in carpet weaving, but in the case the relative share of wages of the child workers is better. The low*

---

[2] Labour Investigation Committee Investigation Committee, Main Report, 1944, p.35.
[3] Report of National Commission on Labour, 1969, p.383.

earnings of the artisan are compensated by the income of his mate, if the latter belongs to the same house. But this is at the cost of education of the junior operative. An artisan cannot afford to educate his wards though education is free. From him an uneducated child is an assets, desire to be educated becomes double liability because of (a) loss of earnings of the child did not work and (b) expenditure on education howsoever small".

In 1978, the Government of India set up a 16-member Committee to examine existing laws, their inadequacies and implementation and also to suggest welfare measures, training and other facilities for the benefits of the children in employment. The Committee, submitted the report suggested, interalia, for raising the minimum age for employment to 15 years.[4]

The Second National Commission on Labour was constituted after three decades in a different backdrop of liberalization, Privatisation and Globalisation (LPG). The Commission was headed by Mr. Ravindra Verma. The Government of India announced the appointment of Commission with twin tasks before them:

i)   to suggest rationalization of existing laws relating to labour in organised sector.

ii)   to suggest an umbrella legislation for ensuring a minimum level of protection to the workers in the unorganised sector.[5]

Initially, when the deliberations on the issue of social security were started, one view was that Commission should confine itself strictly to the matters of security of workers. Consequently, it was realised that the terms of reference is to study and recommend measures for assuring protection and welfare to workers. It has been

---

[4] First Commission on labour was headed by P.B. Gajendragadkar was formed in 1966 to make labour laws consistent with the then dominant discourse of mixed economy. The Commission declared the focus was on improving the living conditions of workers, providing legal protection to the work force, etc.

[5] <http://www.labour.nic.in.comm2/nlc-report.html> accessed on 26th December, 2005.

asked to review the legislation for workers in the organised sector (this includes laws on social security for workers in the organized sector) and also to recommend umbrella legislation that assures protection and welfare of to workers in the unorganised or informal sector.[6] The Commission released its report in the year 2001, which runs upto 1700 pages.

The report discusses in detail plight of children at work place. It further quotes the report on Human Development in South Asia for 1997 which describes the plight of children in South Asian Countries as Follows:[7]

"To be a child in South Asia is to suffer a life of constant denial. Children are often born without their mothers being attended by trained health personnel. Infact, nearly 70% of the mothers struggle alone, surrounded by untrained though anxious relatives at the time of their greatest need. In their survival and development, these children face even more formidable hardies that those they face at birth. Half of the world's malnourished children (83 million) are to be found in just three countries Bangladesh, Pakistan and India. About 85 million children in South Asia have never seen the inside of School. Only half of the total number of school-age children enrolls in schools. Of these 42% drop out before reaching Grade 5. While many children are forced to leave school due to family circumstances and the compulsion to provide economic support to the household at a tender age, one of the main reasons for the high rates school dropout in South Asia is that both parents and children realise the poor quality of education they receive. Dramatic improvements are required in teachers training and supervision in learning material and school facilities. Many children have to work over fifteen hours a day and are after physically abused. Rape and beatings are frequent."

---

[6] *Ibid.*
[7] *Ibid.*

The plights of children, the existing legislation and the schemes of the Government of India has been discussed in detail in the report under a separate chapter on *'woman and child labour'*. The report lays down that there are two perceptions of what constitutes child labour. The first perception identifies Child Labour as work done by children outside their home/family for a minimal wage. According to this perception child labour is synonymous with the exploitation of poor and young child working outside their families. The I.L.O. further supports this view when it says, it is "not concerned with children helping in family farms and doing household chores."It defines child labour to "......include children leading permanently adult lives, working long hours for low wages under conditions damaging to their health and physical and mental development, some times separated from their families, frequently devoid of meaningful educational and training opportunities that could open up a better future to them." The second definition of child labour put forward by groups critical of the conventional definition argues that all forms of work are bad for children.[8] Besides this, the report also lays down that children work in factories and workshops, a number of children are also found in home based work, helping their parents and children work in agricultural sector as well.

The approach of the study group on women and child labour has been that the child, the child's welfare and child's future should be made central in all programmes and in laws also. Every child should have the opportunity to develop his or her skills and potential, to participate both as a citizen and as a worker. The Commission endorses this approach.[9] The entire strategy would have to be based on promoting the norm that no child should work, and all children should be in schools. The Commission observed that the Child Labour (Prohibition & Regulation) Act, 1986 is limited in scope. It does not cover all occupations and processes where children are working. The Act covers only some hazardous occupation and processes. It includes

---

[8] *Ibid.*
[9] *Ibid.*

children working in family based enterprises. The report further emphasized on the issue that the law does not say what should happen to the child labourer once the employer is prosecuted. The report also highlighted for points that the implementation of the Act depends entirely on the State's bureaucratic machinery. It assumes that the bureaucracy, poorly staffed and ill-equipped as it is today, will be able to ensure that children does not work in hazardous processes and occupations, and conditions of work in non-hazardous setting will be upgraded. Education is referred to in three different types of laws. Instead of enabling and empowering parents to send children to school, the report further recommended that the government incorporates the suggestions contained in various judicial pronouncements under relevant laws or guidelines. The Commission also proposed an indicative law on Child Labour, which would replace the existing Child Labour (Regulations and Prohibition) Act, 1986.[10] They have emphasized that a national scheme is to be designed for the payment of children's allowance on universal basis subject to a mean test, to persons below the poverty line. This would be one way of integrating social security schemes with poverty alleviation programmes. Special measures should be taken to prevent sickness and promote the overall well being of children especially the girl child.

The legislative activity revolving around child in this country is more than a century old. But the burden of early legislation was in the area of health, marriage, crime, personal status and to a very minor extent to the employment of the child. With the introduction of factory system in the country, the legislations in the field of regulation of child employment began. The power to legislate in the field of labour relations, labour welfare and vocational and technical training belongs both to the Centre and the States. As such both the Centre and the State legislatures have enacted laws in the field of employment of child labour. However, the State legislations were passed predominantly in the field of non-industrial occupations i.e. shops and commercial establishments.

---

[10] *Ibid.*

In the field of Industrial establishment, the predominant legislative activity has been in the areas of prohibition and regulation of working hours of child labour in certain spheres. The important legislations are Employment of Children Act 1938, Factories Act 1948, Motor Transport Workers Act 1961, Plantation Labour Act 1951, Mines Act 1952, Merchant Shipping Act 1958, Beedi and Cigar Workers (Conditions of Employment) Act, 1966, Child Labour (Prohibition and Regulation) Act, 1986. The key features of briefly different legislation has been discussed.

5.1 Inland Steam Vessels Act, 1917

- Provides provision regulating the employment of children.
- Applies to steam ships ordinarily playing on inland waters.
- Lot of omission due to an old enactment.

5.2 The Children (Pledging of Labour) Act, 1933

The Act was enacted during pre-independence era but remains in force.

- Object of the Act is eradicate the evils rising from pledging the labour of young children.
- An agreement to pledge the labour of children below 15 years by a parent or guardian of a child in return for any payment or benefit is void.[11]
- Act penalize both parent or guardian and employer in case of pledge of labour of the child. Employer is liable for a fine of Rs.200/- [12]and parent or guardian is liable for fine upto Rs.50/-.[13]

---

[11] Section 3, The Children (Pledging of Labour) Act, 1933.
[12] Section 6,*ibid.*
[13] Section 4, *ibid.*

5.3 The Employment of Children Act, 1938:[14]

This is the earliest unrepealed legislation on the statute book controlling the employment of underaged persons in certain types of occupation. It provides:

- No child who has not completed 15 years of age can be employed in any occupation connected with transport of passengers, goods or mail by railways, or a port authority within the limit of a port.[15]
- Limited protection to the children who are within 15-17 years of age. This protection is not applicable to children who are employed as either apprentices or are receiving vocational training.[16]
- Prohibits the employment of children below the age of 14 in workshops connected with bidi-making carpet weaving; cement manufacturing, cloth printing, dyeing and weaving, manufacturing of matches, explosives and fire works, mica cutting and splitting, shellac manufacture, soap manufacture, taning and wool cleaning.
- The State Governments are empowered to extend the scope of this provision to any other employment.[17] In exercise of this power Government of Madras has extended the Act to children working as cleaners in workshops attached to motor companies. The Government of Uttar Pradesh has extended the provisions of the Act to brass ware and glass bangle industries.
- The penalty for the breach of the Act is imprisonment upto one month or fine upto Rs.500/- or both.[18]

It is however imperative to mention here that this Act has been repealed to the extent it is inconsistent with the Child Labour (Prohibition and Regulation) Act, 1986.[19]

---

[14] The Employment of Children Act, 1938, Act No.XXVI of 1938.
[15] Section 3(3), *ibid.*
[16] Section 3(2), ibid.
[17] Section 3-A, *ibid.*
[18] Section 4, *ibid.*
[19] For the provisions of the Child Labour (Prohibition and Regulation) Act, 1966 see *infra 5.2.13.*

5.4 The Factories Act, 1948:

The first Welfare Legislation passed by the Britishers was Factories Act, 1881. The implementation of the Act was restricted:

- It only applies to those establishments where one hundred or more persons are employed.
- Minimum age was seven years.
- Successive employment on the same day was prohibited.
- Duration of employment i.e. working hours was not to exceed nine hours a day and at least four holidays in a month.

The Act was amended in 1891 to increase the minimum age upto nine years.

The Act was again amended in 1948 and the key features are as follows:[20]

- Prohibits the employment of children below 14 years of age in factory.[21]
- Factory covers the establishment, which employs 10 or more workers with the aid of power or 20 or more workers without the aid of power.[22]
- Persons who are between the 14 and 15 years, they can be employed under following restrictions provided under Section 68, 69 and 71 of the Act:
- Such persons should have certificate of fitness issued by a Surgeon and should carry a token giving a reference to such certificate.[23]
- The certifying Surgeon should follow the procedure laid down in Section 69.
- They should not work at night i.e. 12 consecutive hours including the period from 10 PM to 6 AM.[24]

---

[20] Act No.39 of 1948.
[21] Section 67, The Factories Act, 1948.
[22] Section 2(m), *ibid.*
[23] Section 68, *ibid.*
[24] Section 71(i)(6), *ibid.*

- They should not work for more than four and half hours a day.[25]
- The period of work should be limited to two shifts.[26]
- The shift should not overlap.[27]
- Spread over should not to exceed five hours and should also not change except once in 30 days.[28]
- Prohibits successive employment on the same day.[29]
- Employer should display a notice regarding the periods of work for such children.[30]
- Manager should mention register in respect of such child-workers.[31]
- No child is to be employed except in accordance with the notice of periods of work displayed.[32]
- State Government is empowered to make rules prescribing the physical standards to be attained by children and adolescents working in factories.[33]

5.5. The Plantation Labour Act, 1951[34]

- Covers all tea, coffee, rubber and cinchona plantation admeasuring 5 hectares or where 15 persons or more are employed on any days of the preceding 12 months.[35]
- State Government is empowered to extend the provisions of the Act to any land measuring less than 5 hectares or the person employed is less than 15.
- No child and no adolescent shall be employed for work unless he is certified fit for work by a Surgeon.[36]

---

[25] Section 71(1)(a), *ibid.*
[26] Section 72, *ibid.*
[27] *Ibid.*
[28] *Ibid.*
[29] Section 71(4), *ibid.*
[30] Section 72, *ibid.*
[31] Section 73, *ibid.*
[32] Section 74, *ibid.*
[33] Section 76(b), *ibid.*
[34] Act No.69 of 1951.
[35] Section 4(a), *ibid.*
[36] Section 26, *ibid.*

- Certificate is valid only for one year.[37]
- Use of false certificate is punishable by imprisonment which may extend to one month or with fine or both.[38]

Act is comprehensive as it is the only Act which makes the provisions for education as a responsibility of employer and so is for the housing, medical and recreational facilities.[39]

5.6 The Mines Act, 1952[40]

The scope of Mines Act is limited.

- Applies to excavation where operation for the purpose of searching for or obtaining minerals has been or is carried out.[41]
- Not only prohibits the employment of any 'child'[42] but even presence of a child in any part of mine which is below ground or in any open cast working in which mining operation is carried on.[43]
- Adolescent who has completed the age of sixteen years is allowed to work only if he has a medical certificate of fitness for work.[44]
- Certificate is valid for 12 months only.[45]

5.7 The Merchant Shipping Act, 1958

- Prohibits the employment of children in any capacity, who are below 15 years of age on sea going except:[46]

    a) in a school ship or training ship; or

    b) in a ship in which all persons employed are members of one   family; or

---

[37] Section 27(2), *ibid.*
[38] Section 34, *ibid.*
[39] Section 5, 6 7, *ibid.*
[40] Act No.35 of 1952.
[41] Section 2(j), *ibid.*
[42] Child means a person who has not completed 15 years.
[43] Section 45(i), *ibid.*
[44] Section 40(i), *ibid.*
[45] Section 41(i), *ibid.*
[46] Section 109, The Merchant Shipping Act, 1958.

c) in a home made ship of less than two hundred tons gross; or

d) where such person is employed on nominal wages and will be in charge of his father or other adult near male relative

- Act applies only to ships registered in India.[47]
- Government is empowered to make rules regarding the employment of young persons.[48]

5.8   The Apprentice Act, 1961

- Object of the Act is to provide for the regulation and control of training of apprentices in trade and for matters connected therewith.[49]
- 'Apprentice' is a person who is going apprenticeship training in a designated trade in pursuance of contract of apprenticeship.[50]
- No person is qualified for being engaged as an apprentice to undergo training unless he has completed the age of 14 years and satisfies the others standards of physical fitness and education as may be prescribed.[51]
- If the apprentice is minor his guardian is required to enter into a contract of apprenticeship with the employer and it shall be registered with Apprenticeship Advisor.[52]

5.9   The Motor Transport Workers Act, 1961[53]

- Covers every motor transport undertaking employing 5 or more transport workers.[54]
- State Government is empowered to extend the provisions of the Act to any motor transport undertakings employing less than 5 workers.[55]

---

[47] Section 2, *ibid.*
[48] Ibid.
[49] The Apprentices Act, 1961, Preamble.
[50] Section 2(aa), *ibid.*
[51] Section 3, *ibid.*
[52] Section 4(i), *ibid.*
[53] Act No.27 of 1961.
[54] Section 1(4), The Motor Transport Workers Act, 1961.
[55] Section 1(4), *ibid.*

- Prohibits the employment of children below the age of 15 years in the motor transport undertaking.[56]
- Adolescents are prohibited to work unless certified by a Surgeon.[57]
- Certificate is valid for 12 months only.[58]

5.10 The Beedi and Cigar Works (Conditions of Employment) Act, 1966

Though the Factories Act, 1948 apply to workers engaged in beedi manufacturing yet there had been a tendency on the part of the employers to split the concern into smaller units to escape the provisions of the Act.

- No child below the age of 14 years is allowed to work in any industrial premises.[59]
- Employment of young persons between 14 to 18 years is prohibited between 7 PM to 6 AM.[60]
- Penalties for the breach of provision is imprisonment upto three months or fine upto Rs.500/- or both.[61]
- Provisions for Canteen,[62] First aid[63] cleaning[64] and ventilation[65] are also made under the Act.

5.11 The Shops and Commercial Establishment Act, 1969

Provisions relating to minimum age also exist in different state shops and commercial establishment Act.

---

[56] Section 21, *ibid.*
[57] Section 22, *ibid.*
[58] Section 23(2), *ibid.*
[59] Beedi and Cigar Works (Conditions of Employment) Act, 1966, Section 24(b).
[60] Section 25, *ibid.*
[61] Section 32, *ibid.*
[62] Section 16, *ibid.*
[63] Section 15, *ibid.*
[64] Section 8, *ibid.*
[65] Section 9, *ibid.*

- Applies to shops, commercial establishment, restaurants and hotels and place of amusement and notified areas to which Factories Act does not apply.
- State Government is empowered to extend the coverage of the Act in any establishment.
- Minimum age of employment is 12 years in Bihar, Gujarat, J&K, Madhya Pradesh, Karntaka, Orissa, Rajasthan, Tripura, Uttar Pradesh, West Bengal, Goa, Daman & Diu and Manipur.[66]
- Age is 14 years in Andhra Pradesh, Assam, Haryana, Himachal Pradesh, Kerala, Tamil Nadhu, Punjab, Delhi, Chandigarh, Pondichery and Meghalaya.[67]
- Minimum age of employment is 15 years in Maharashtra.[68]
- No separate Act in Andaman Nicobar, Arunachal Pradesh, Dadra and Nagar Haveli, Lakshdweep, Nagaland and Sikkim.[69]

5.12 Radiation Protection Rules, 1971

- Children below 18 years are not to be employed where radiation exists.

5.13 The Child Labour (Prohibition and Regulation) Act, 1986

The Act is an outcome of various recommendations made by a series of Committees.[70] There was a constant demand in favour of a uniform comprehensive legislation to prohibit the engagement of children in certain other employments to achieve this goal, parliament enacted the Child Labour (Prohibition and Regulation) Act, 1986 (CLPRA) which came into force on 23 December 1986. The objectives of Child Labour (Prohibition and Regulation) Act, 1986 are:

---

[66] See *Child Labour in India*, Document 4(1979), The Indian Journal of Public Administration, Vol.XXV (No.3), p.933.
[67] *Ibid.*
[68] *Ibid.*
[69] *Ibid.*
[70] The National Commission on Labour, 1969, The Committee on Child Labour, 1979, the Gurupadswamy Committee on Child Labour 1976 and the Mehta Committee, 1984.

- Banning the employment of children i.e. those who have not completed their fourteenth year, in specified occupation and processes.
- Laying down procedures to decide modifications to the schedule of banned occupation or processes.
- Regulating the conditions of work of children in employment where they are not prohibited from working.
- Laying down enhanced penalties for employment of children in violation of the provisions of this Act and other Acts which forbid the employment of children.

The significant provisions of the Act are as under:

- Prohibits the employment of any person who has not completed his fourteenth year of age[71] in occupations and processes set forth in Part-A[72] and Part-B[73] of the schedule of the Act.
- Act classifies the establishments in two categories i.e. first one is where the child labour is prohibited and second one is where the working conditions of child shall be regulated.[74]
- Central Government has power to amend the schedule.[75]
- Child Labour Technical Advisory Committee is constituted for the purpose of addition of occupations and processes of the schedule.[76]
- Prohibition of employment is not applicable where process is carried on by an occupier with the aid of his family or school established by or recognized or receiving assistance from Government.[77]

---

[71] Section 3 provide 'No Child shall be employed or permitted to work in any occupations set forth in Part A of the Schedule or in any workshop wherein, any of the processes set forth in Part B of the Schedule is carried on'.

[72] Part-A of the Schedule of the Act specifies 13 Occupation in which employment of children is not allowed.

[73] Part-B of the schedule of Act specifies 54 processes in which employment of children is allowed where the process is carried out by the occupier with the aid of his family or to any school established by or receiving assistance or recognition from Government.

[74] Section 3, The Child Labour (Prohibition and Regulation) Act, 1986.

[75] Section 4, *ibid.*

[76] Section 5, *ibid.*

- Provides provisions for regulation of conditions of work of children in establishment which are not referred in schedule.[78]
- Appropriate Government is empowered to make rules for the health and safety of the children employed.[79]
- In case of dispute as to the age of a child the certificate granted by a prescribed medical authority is conclusive evidence.[80]
- Any person, Police Officer or Inspector may file a complaint of the commission of an offence under the Act.[81]
- No Court inferior to that of Metropolitan Magistrate or a Magistrate of the first class shall try any offence under this Act.[82]
- Penalties are stringent, any person who employs any child in any hazardous employment shall be punishable with imprisonment for a term not less than 3 months but which may extends to one year or with fine not less than Rs.10,000/- but which may extend to Rs.20,000/- or with both.[83]
- For a repeated offence, the imprisonment for a term which shall not be less than six months but which may extend to two years.[84]
- For violation of any other provisions under the Act or rules, the punishment is imprisonment which may extend to one month, or with fine which may extend to Rs.10,000/- rupees or both.[85]

The Act provides both for imprisonment and fine but in practice, there are few instances where the employer is prosecuted, he is generally fined. The CLPRA 1986 increases and makes more stringent penalties for employing child labour in violation in comparison to Factories, Mines, Merchant Shipping and Motor Transport Acts. It

---

[77] Proviso to Section 3, *ibid.*
[78] Section 7, *ibid.*
[79] Section 13, *ibid.*
[80] Section 10, *ibid.*
[81] Section 16(1), *ibid.*
[82] Section 16(3), *ibid.*
[83] *Ibid.*
[84] Section 14(2), *ibid.*
[85] Section 14(3), *ibid.*

empowers the Union Government to bring into force provisions that regulate conditions of work of children in non-hazardous occupations. It provides the machinery i.e. child Labour Technical Advisory Committee for adding to the list of occupations and processes in which employment of child is prohibited. The ban has been imposed by the Labour Ministry on the employment of children as domestic servants or servants or in dhabas, restaurants, motels, tea shops, resorts, spas or in other recreational centres. The decision has been taken on the recommendation of Child Labour Technical Advisory Committee and will be effective from 10th October, 2006.[86] The Committee while recommending a ban said that these children are at times even subject to sexual abuse. The incidents of these kids either go unnoticed and unreported as they take place in close confines of the household or dhabas or restaurant. This measure is expected to go a long way in ameliorating the conditions of hapless working children.[87]

But still the Act needs amendment for better implementation and enforcement. According to Neera Burra,[88] there are number of loopholes in the Act. She has further also tried to show how unpracticable and unrealistic it is to draw a distinction between hazardous and non-hazardous processes in a particular industry.[89] One of the prominent loophole is that child can continue to work if they are a part of family of labour. It covers only 10 percent of total working children, which are working in organized Sector. Moreover, the agricultural sector, which constitutes more than 75 percent of the child employment, is not covered under the Act. The risk is more in case of agricultural Sector because of pesticide exposure. The organs of the children are still developing, they are less able than adults to expel toxins from their body. Their breathing rate is much higher than adults and they have more skin surface per unit of body weight than adults, allowing them to both breathe in and absorb higher concentrations of toxins. Infact, there should be prohibition on all forms of child

---

[86] <http://www.newkerala.com/news4php?action=fullnew&id=170> accessed on 2nd August, 2012.
[87] Ibid.
[88] Quoted in M.C. Mehta v. State of Tamil Nadu AIR 1997 SC 699.
[89] Ibid, p.708

labour since all occupations are hazardous and affect development of child if the child is denied primary, elementary education because of the need to work, it is a hazard in itself.[90]

The problem of child labour can hardly be solved by rising the minimum age of child to 15 as suggested by Committee on Child Welfare. It is submitted, that unless basic needs are provided to all people which, includes food, shelter, clothing, educational facilities, the root cause cannot be eradicated only by prohibiting the employment of children and raising the minimum age of employment. There is no uniformity in the labour holidays, leave, safety and welfare of child labour. In view of8 this, it is suggested that a comprehensive legislation on child labour be enacted which should apply to children employed in industrial establishment. This would bring uniformity of standards in all industries in the sphere of employment of children. There is no labour legislation which seeks to regulate working hours, holiday, leave, health and welfare in domestic services, unorganized sectors and to casual labour. The circumstances suggested that there should be comprehensive legislation for child labour employed in rural and. unorganised sectors. However, in making such legislation it is necessary to keep in mind the practical difficulties and problems of enforcement.

---

[90] Ossie Fernandes Towards Amendments/Restricting of the Child Labour Prohibition & Regulation Act, 1986, a draft note prepared on behalf of the Legal Working Group Campaign Against Child Labour (CACL)

CHAPTER VII
JUDICIARY: PILLIAR TO STREGHTEN CHILD RIGHTS

Judiciary in our country has shown a keen interest in the conditions of working children. In the well known *Asiad Project[1]* the Apex Court held that *Article 24* of the Constitution, which even if not followed up by appropriate legislation, must operate *proprio vigore* and construction work is included in the hazardous occupations. Therefore, there can be no doubt that even if the construction industry in not mentioned as hazardous activity in the schedule to the Employment of Children Act, 1938, no child below fourteen years can be employed in the construction work. Further, in another case the Hon'ble Supreme Court observed that it not enough merely to identify and release bonded labourers but it is equally perhaps more, important that after identification and release, they must be rehabilitated, because without rehabilitation, they would be driven by poverty, helplessness and despair into serfdom once again.[2] In *labourers working on Salal Hydro Project v. State of Jammu and Kashmir and others[3]* the Hon'ble Apex Court directed that whenever the Central Government undertakes a construction project which is likely to last for a considerable period of time, it should ensure that children of construction workers who are living at or near the project site are given facilities for schooling. The Court also specified that this may be done either by the Central Government itself, or if the Central Government entrusts the project work or any part thereof to a contractor, necessary provision to this effect may be made in the contract with the contractor. In *Rajangam, Secretary, District Beedi Workers Union v. State of Tamil Nadu and others.[4]* The Supreme Court observed that tobacco manufacturing was indeed hazardous occupation to the health of children. Child labour in this trade should

---

[1] *Peoples Union Democratic Rights v. Union of India,* AIR 1982, SC 1473, wherein it was contended that the Employment of Children Act, 1938 was not applicable in case of Projects in Delhi since construction industry was not a process specified in the schedule of Children Act, 1938.

[2] Bandhua Mukti Morcha v. Union of India & others, AIR 1984, SC 802, Bandhua Mukti Morcha is an organization working for the release of bonded labourers. In this case also the Apex Court considered the scope and ambit of Article 23 in detail.

[3] AIR 1994 SC 177, Also see this case *infra* Chapter 5.1.

[4] (1992) 1 SCC 221.

therefore, be prohibited as far as possible and employment of child labour should be stopped immediately or in a phased manner that is to be decided by the State Government but it should be a period not exceeding three years.

In **M.C. Mehta v. State of Tamil Nadu & others**[5] case M.C. Mehta, a noted environmentalist and social activist, whose contribution in the area of protection and conservation of the environment has been internationally acclaimed, filed a public interest litigation in 1986 against the harrowing practices of employing children in the match, fireworks and explosive factories of Sivakasi in Kamrajar district of Tamil Nadu. A three Judge Bench of the Supreme Court comprising Justice Kuldip Singh, Justice B.L. Hansaria and Justice S.B. Majumdar delivered a landmark judgment on 10 December, 1996. The Court gave certain directions regarding the payment of compensation and thought that an advocate committee should visit the area and made a comprehensive report relating to the various aspects of the matter, as mentioned in order of August 14, 1991. The Committee was to consist of (i) Sh. R.K. Jain, a Senior Advocate; (ii) Ms. Indira Jaisingh, another Senior Advocate; and (iii) Sh. K.C. Dua, Advocate. The Committee has done a commendable job. It submitted its report on 11.11.1991 containing many recommendations. The Court gave the following principal directions:

1.   In fulfillment of the legislative intention behind the enactment of the Child Labour (Prohibition and Regulation) Act, 1986, every offending employer must be asked to pay compensation amounting to Rs.20,000/- for every child employed in contravention of the provisions of the Act.[6]

2.   The inspectors appointed under Section 17 of the Act should see that the compensation is paid, and deposited in a fund to be called 'Child Labour

---

[5] AIR 1997 SC 699 In *M.C. Mehta v. State of Tamil Nadu and others AIR 1991 SC 283*. In this case Supreme Court allowed the children to be employed in the process of packing of fire works but packing should be done in an area away from the place of manufacture to avoid exposure to accident.
[6] *Ibid*, para 27.

Rehabilitation-cum-Welfare Fund'. The liability of the employer will not cease even if she/he desires to disengage the child presently employed.[7]

3.   It would be appropriate to have such a fund district wise or area-wise. The Fund so generated shall form a corpus whose income shall be used only for the concerned child. The quantum could be the income earned on the corpus deposited qua the child. To maximize the income, the amount can be deposited in a high yielding scheme of any nationalized bank or other public body.[8]

4.   As this income will be insufficient to dissuade the parent/guardian from seeking employment for the child, the State should discharge its obligation to cover the short fall. As such, one adult member of the family whose child is employed in a factory or a mine or in any other hazardous work should get a job anywhere in lieu of that of the child. As a large number of working children are engaged in such occupations, asking the respective State government to assure alternative employment to an adult would strain the resources of the states. As such, where it is not possible to provide a job to an adult member of the family, the government concerned should, as its contribution/grant of Rs.5000/- per child in the child labour Rehabilitation-cum-Welfare Fund.[9]

5.   A survey should be conducted of the type of child labour under issue which should be completed within six months starting 10 December, 1996. To begin with, the survey could be taken up in relation to Article 24, which might be regarded as the basis for determining which hazardous aspect of employment should be treated as the criterion, the most hazardous form of employment being ranked the highest priority, and others similarly prioritized in terms of hazardous entailed.[10]

---

[7] *Ibid.*
[8] *Ibid.*
[9] *Id,* para 28, 29 and 30.
[10] *Id ,* para 31(1) and 31(2).

6. The employment provided to an able bodied adult could be in the industry where the child is employed or a public undertaking, and would be manual in nature in as much as the child in question must have been engaged in doing manual work. The undertaking chosen for employment shall be one that is nearest to the place where the family lives.[11]

7. In case where alternative employment cannot be made available the parent/guardian of the concerned child should be paid the income earned as interest on the corpus of Rs.25,000/- for each child every month. The employment given or payment made would cease to be operative if the child is not sent to school by the parent/guardian.[12]

8. On discontinuation of the employment of the child, free education should be assured in a suitable institution with a view to making him a better citizen. Article 45 of the Constitution mandates compulsory education for all citizen until they complete the age of fourteen. It would be the duty of the inspectors to ensure that this direction of the Constitution is complied with.[13]

9. A district would be the unit of the collection with its executive head keeping a watchful eye on the work of the inspectors. Also in view of the magnitude of the task a separate cell in the labour department of the appropriate government should be created. The operation of the scheme would need to be monitored, and this could perhaps be undertaken by the secretary of the department, and overall monitoring by the Ministry of Labour would be beneficial and worthwhile.[14]

---

[11] *Id*, para 31(3) and 31(4).
[12] *Id*, para 31(5).
[13] *Id, para* 31(6).
[14] *Id*, para 31(7).

10. The Secretary to the Ministry of Labour should apprise the Supreme Court within one year, starting from 10 December, 1996 regarding compliance with the directions.[15]

Detailed guidelines were forwarded to the State governments on 26th December, 1996 indicating the manner in which the directions of the Supreme Court could be given effect to. The first phase of survey was completed by all the State governments/UTs except in Nagaland. The Ministry of Labour had sanctioned a sum of Rs.8 Crore for the purpose. The State governments, where employment of child labour in hazardous occupations was found, had already initiated steps for the constitution of the Child Labour Rehabilitation-cum-Welfare Funds at the district level. The amount of compensation received statewise from the offending employers was is given below:[16]

	State	Rupees
i)	Andhra Pardesh	40,000
ii)	Haryana	80,000
iii)	Karnataka	60,000
iv)	Madhya Pradesh	20,000
v)	Maharashtra	2,00,000
vi)	Orissa	1,00,000
vii)	Punjab	1,20,000
viii)	West Bengal	80,000

State governments/UT administration of Andhra Pradesh, Chandigarh, Dadra & Nagar Haveli, Daman & Diu, Goa, Haryana, Karnataka, Kerala, Madhya Pradesh, Maharashtra, Mizoram, Orissa, Pondicherry, Punjab, Tamil Nadu, Uttar Pradesh and West Bengal have reported that separate labour cells have been constituted to ensure

---

[15] *Id*, para 31(8).
[16] Lakshmidhar Mishra, *Child Labour in India*, (Oxford University Press, New Delhi, 2000), p.230.

the enforcement of various provision of the Child Labour (Prohibition and Regulation) Act, 1986.

In another significant judgment given by the Apex Court on the basis of PIL a number of directions on the identification release and rehabilitation of child labour has also been given.[17] The Court, interalia, directed the Government of India to convene a meeting with the State Government to evolve principles/policies for progressive elimination of employment of children below 14 years in all employments consistent with the scheme laid down in Civil Writ Petition No.465/86. These directions were given by the Court in the context of employment of children in the Carpet Industries in the State of Uttar Pradesh. In this case the Court issued the following directions to the Government of Uttar Pradesh:

1.   Investigate the conditions of employment of children.
2.   Issue such welfare directions as are appropriate for total prohibition of employment below 14 years of age.
3.   Provides facilities for education, health, sanitation, nutritious food etc.

The implementation of the directions of the Supreme Court is being mentioned by the Ministry of Labour and compliance thereof was reported to the Court on the basis of information received from the State/UT Government.[18]

In *Bachpan Bachao Andolan vs. Union of India and Others*[19] the Supreme Court observed directed that keeping in view the infrastructural limitation, the labour Department to begin implementing the Delhi Action Plan by accommodating for the time being about 500 children every month. The Court observed that the Delhi Action Plan which provides a detailed procedure for interim care and protection of the rescued children to be followed by Labour Department as prepared by the National Commission with the modifications mentioned in the judgment and we further direct

---

[17] *Bandhua Mukti Morcha v. Union of India and others,* AIR 1997 SC 2218.
[18] Annual Report, 1999-2000, Ministry of Labour, GOI, p. 164.
[19] WP (Crl) 82 of 2009 Order dated 24th December, 2010

all the authorities concerned to immediately implement the same. The Government of NCT of Delhi through the Labour Department is directed to file its First Taken Report to this Court after six months.

In another important case *Bachpan Bachao Andolan v. Union of India*,[20] in this case the Supreme Court of India has directed the government to ban the employment of children in the country's circus industry. Until recently, the form of entertainment was exempt from the laws which state that no child under the age of 14 can be placed into labor. However, an amendment passed to bring circuses in line with other industries has been ignored by employers and now the government has been encouraged to impose a complete ban. We plan to deal with the problem of children's exploitation systematically. In this order we are limiting our directions regarding children working in the Indian Circuses:

(i) In order to implement the fundamental right of the children under Article 21A it is imperative that the Central Government must issue suitable notifications prohibiting the employment of children in circuses within two months from today.

(ii) The respondents are directed to conduct simultaneous raids in all the circuses to liberate the children and check the violation of fundamental rights of the children. The rescued children are kept in the Care and Protective Homes till they attain the age of 18 years.

(iii) The respondents are also directed to talk to the parents of the children and in case they are willing to take their children back to their homes, they may be directed to do so after proper verification.

(iv) The respondents are directed to frame proper scheme of rehabilitation of rescued children from circuses.

(v) We direct the Secretary of Ministry of Human Resources Development, Department of Women and Child Development to file a comprehensive affidavit of compliance within ten weeks.

---

[20] Writ Petition (C) No.51 OF 2006 Judgment delivered on 18 April, 2011.

CHAPTER VIII

CHILD LABOUR: A PARADIGM SHIFT IN APPROACHES

"I am the child.

All the world waits for my coming.

All the earth watches with interest to see what I become.

Civilization hangs in the balance.

For what I am, the world of tomorrow will be.

I am the child.

You hold in your hand my destiny.

You determine, largely, whether I shall succeed or fail,

Give me, I pray you, these things that make for happiness.

Train me, I beg you, that I may be a blessing to the world".

Mamie Gene Cole[1]

It may be said that the aforesaid appeal lies at the back of the saying that *"child is the father of man"*. To enable fathering of a valiant and vibrant man, the child must be groomed well in the formative years of his life. He must receive education; acquire knowledge of man and materials and blossom in such an atmosphere that on reaching age, he is found to be a man with a mission, a man who matters so far as the society is concerned.[2]

India, the Union of twenty-eight States and seven Union Territories, is a socialist, Secular and Democratic Republic. The Indian constitution envisages a parliamentary form of government and is federal in nature with some unitary features. The size and population of some of India's largest states is comparable to some countries in Europe, Africa, Latin America or Asia. India continues to wage its battle against poverty, and its attendant, such as, high morality rates, malnutrition and

---

[1] Quoted in M.C. Mehta v. State of Tamil Nadu AIR 1997 SC 701.
[2] *Ibid.*

illiteracy, the greatest victims of which are children and women.[3] India has 400 million children below the age of eighteen years, the largest child population in the world.[4] The importance of child has now widely been recognized in the Convention on the Rights of Child, 1989 also. The Government of India submitted its first country Report on the Convention on the Rights of the Child in February 1997 which stated that:[5]

'Unless the life of the child in the family and community improves, all development efforts would be meaningless. There is, therefore, a need to raise awareness and create an ethos of respect for the rights of the child in society to meet his or her basic development needs. Advocacy and social mobilization are two crucial processes which are being emphasized to achieve this end. With India's ratification of the UN Convention on the Rights of the Child, the 'rights approach' to child development is gradually gaining importance and will henceforth form the basis of Government's strategy towards child development.'

There has been a paradigm shift in approaches towards children. The shift in focus is from the welfare to the developmental approach.[6]

Earlier Approach	Present Approach
Needs	Rights
Welfare	Development
Institutional and residential care	Non-residential and family based alternatives.
Custodial care	Holistic development

---

[3] Convention on the Rights of the Child: India First periodic Report- 2001 available at http://www.wcd.nic.in/crc.htm accessed on 15th September, 2013.
[4] *Ibid.*
[5] *India Country Report on the Convention of the Rights of the Child,* Government of India, 1997.
[6] Asha Bajpai, *Child Rights in India Law, Policy and Practice ,* (Oxford University Press, New Delhi, 2003) p.438.

Segregation and isolation	Inclusion in mainstream
Beneficiary and recipient	Participant and partner.

In the last decade, we have witnessed a tremendous progress in the areas of literacy, especially female literacy and women employment. Neera Burra, a social activist, has observed that if there is at all blue print for tackling the problem of child labour, it is education.[7] In Kerala the labour, participation of child is less as compare to all India estimates. This is due to higher literacy rate in Kerala as compare to whole of India. The fundamental right to education for children in the age group 6-14 years has been inserted in the Constitution by Eighty-Sixth Amendment Act, 2002.

Child labour is another major problem faced by India, which is also directly related to the child. If the literacy rate is high then there can be decrease in child labour because the educated people can better understand and differentiate between sending children to work and to school. As there has been several labours legislation enacted alongwith Article 24 of the Constitution of India which prohibits the employment of children in mines, factories and hazardous industries, which has been explained earlier are also not free from defects which are briefly pointed out as under:

The Child Labour (Prohibition and Regulation) Act, 1986 was enacted with the intention to ban the employment of children in specified occupation and processes. But the Act failed to the fulfill the objective desired due of following reasons:-

- The Act fails to cover the unorganized sector where 75 percent of the children are employed.

---

[7] See *Supra* note 1, p.709.

- The word 'hazardous' has not been defined and is left to the Child Labour Technical Advisory Committee to define hazardous occupations and processes.

- Section 3 of the Child Labour (Prohibition and Regulation) Act, 1986 legalises employment of children where the occupation, work or processes is carried on by the occupier with the aid of his family.

- Employers, Trade Union and Corporate Sector can play a positive role to deal with this problem. There is need to create awareness in the society towards the hazards caused to child by labour.

- The Labour Ministry notification has imposed a ban on the employment of children as a domestic help, restaurants, hotels, motels and dhabas. The ban is going to be effective from October 10, 2006.[8] The child employers have made a mockery of this ban in Bangalore by using Rs.20 affidavit to convert a 12 year child into an adult.[9] The intentions of the government are good, but there has to be effective surveillance and proper rehabilitation of these children.

As a commitment towards children, the Government of India has set up the Department of Women and Child Development in 1985. The creation of a separate Department was a landmark step in bringing *Child Rights* to the centre-stage. Another positive step in this regard was accession to the Convention on the Rights of Child in 1992. While acceding to the CRC,[10] India had declared with regard to Article 32 that

"While fully subscribing to the objectives and purposes of the Convention, realizing that certain rights of the child, namely, those pertaining to the economic, social and cultural rights can only be progressively implemented in developing countries, subject to the extent of available resources and within the framework of international co-operation, recognizing that the child has to be protected from exploitation of all forms, including economic exploitation;

---

[8] <http:// www.timesofindia.indiatimes.com/articleshow/1838656.cms> accessed on August 4, 2012.
[9] *The Times of India*, October 16,2006, Rs 20 affidavit makes 12 -yr-olds into adults in Bangalore, p. 6.
[10] Convention on the Rights of the Child, 1989.

nothing that for several reasons, children of different ages work in India; having prescribed minimum wages for employment in hazardous occupations and in certain areas; having made regulatory provisions regarding hours and conditions of employment, and being aware that it is not practical immediately to prescribe minimum ages for admission to each and every areas of employment in India – the GOI undertakes measures to progressively implement the provisions of Article 32, particularly paragraph 2(a), in accordance with its national legislation and relevant international instruments to which it is a State Party."[11]

It is note worthy that in the last three decades several major policies and action plans have been announced for improving the status of children which have already been discussed. But still the commitment undertaken by India require that legislative administrative and other measures follow to implement specific policies and a review and revision of all pertaining laws to the children. The following are suggestions which can combat the problem of violation of *Child labour* in India.

Education is considered as an important human right endeavour to sustain life with dignity. Though, the education has become a fundamental right with the 86th Constitutional Amendment Act. The Right of Children to Free and Compulsory Education Act, 2009 is full of lacunas. This is the right time for the government to redraft the Bill on the basis of Common School System and get it legislated at the earliest. There is also a need of a strong political will to ensure free, equitable and quality education to children.

Many human rights can only be accessed through education which operates as a multiplier enhancing the enjoyment of all individual rights and freedoms.[12] Education has to be made accessible flexible and above all priority must be given to the quality

---

[11]See *Supra* note 3.
[12] Kartarina Tomasevski, *The Right to Education – a discussion source: International Development Cooperation Agency* <http://www.sida.org.> accessed on 1st June, 2013.

of education. Education System should be supported by national programmes that provide resources for incentive, income generation and other means that can support the families of the children.

- *Educate a boy child, educate a person,*
  Educate a girl, educate a family.[13]

In our partriachal society, educating a girl child has other benefits also. An educated woman, when she becomes a mother nurtures the child and gives him or her values that sustain development. This will also adversely affect the maternal mortality rate and infant mortality rate. Our imperative should be to build an environment which focuses on the rights of girl child in totality where the girls are given freedom and opportunity to grow and develop as a responsible child citizen of tomorrow. This is because today educated girl child is tomorrow's empowered women.[14]

Mass awareness drives are necessary for educating people about the correct age of marriage, need of girl child education and against son preference, prenatal sex determination and sex-selection, violence and abuse against girls and the commercial exploitation of children, the dangers of early child bearing, and the prevention of HIV/AIDS.[15]

A Child Labour Vigilance Committee should be formed at panchayat level, comprising local NGOs, Panchayat members and child representative. The Community, Law enforcement officials, teachers and personnel involved in the child labour elimination programme need to be sensitized on the *Child Rights* and protection. In child labour intensive districts, employment opportunities for adults have to be stepped up. Families below the poverty line should be attached to self-help

---

[13] Quoted in Shalu Nigam, *Education and empowerment of the Girl Child: A Legal Perspective,* Legal News & Views, December, 2001, p.9.
[14] *Ibid.*
[15] See *Supra* note 3.

groups or other income-generating schemes so that they can improve their economic situation. There should be separate policy for providing social security and services of education and health to the children of families below the poverty line. Existing poverty alleviation programmes and adult employment schemes have to be co-ordinated and linked to efforts for the elimination of child labour.

In an order at ameliorating conditions of hapless working children, the Government has already ordered ban on employment of children as domestic, help, or servants or in dhabas, restaurants, hotels and motels, teashops, resort, spas or in other recreational centres, which has come into effect from October 10, 2006. The decision has been taken on the recommendation of Technical Advisory Committee on child labour.[16] The Committee has further emphasized that in these occupations children are subjected to psychological traumas, sexual abuse and drug abuse also.[17] But how far this law is successful depends on the rehabilitation programme initiated by the government.[18] These types of initiative taken by the government were welcomed by all NGOs and society also. If a strong political will is created the realization of *Child Rights* no longer remains a difficult task.

The media has a large role to play in mobilizing public support and involvement for preventing *Child Rights* violations. Due to its wide outreach and its ability to mould public opinion, it is a powerful tool for social change. Therefore, there is a need for involving a media in a sustained manner. The media in many countries have played a pivotal role in creating awareness of the Convention on the Rights of the Child and other legislation. The media could also play a pivotal role in the actual implementation of the rights of the child. It is also important that media themselves do not abuse children. The integrity of the child should be protected in

---

[16] <http://www.newkerala.com/news4.php?action=fullnews&id=110> accessed on August 6th , 2012.
[17] *Ibid.*
[18] Even the Assistant Labour Commissioner, Chandigarh, who is responsible for the implementation of this Act, is not clear what she would do if labour inspector were to rescue child from any of the places mentioned in the law. There has not been proper co-ordination or communication on the matter between the Labour Department and the Social Welfare Department of UT Administration. *The Tribune* October 13, 2006.

reporting about the involvement of child criminal activities, sexual abuse and family problems.

The corporate sector can also play an important and positive role to deal with the problem of child labour. During 1990's large business concern throughout the world came under pressure to pay greater attention to the impact that their activities were having on the environment and human rights of their work force i.e. labourers. The Corporate Social Responsibility (CSR) movement is a response by employers on the above mentioned concerns only. The trends in 1990s were in the direction of self-regulation and voluntary codes of conduct concentrated on particular sector such as garments, sporting goods, foot wear, toys, agricultural products, Mining etc.[19]

The employer organization can play a significant role in influency their member enterprise to ensure that no child labour is used on their premises. They can also encourage their member to go step further by taking measures to ensure that their suppliers and contractors in the informal economy also do not use child labour.[20]

There is a need to make the Government functionaries, NGOs and professionals working with children more aware about the Convention on the Right of Child (CRC). CRC should be made part of the school curriculum and school children should be involved in dissemination of information about *Child Rights* through child to child and child to community activities. *Child Rights* should also be included in curriculum of all colleges as well as in professional training of all those who work with children or provide services to them. Awareness of CRC should percolate down to grass roots level through greater participation and partnerships. Government should forge a partnership with NGOs and media to spread awareness

---

[19] <http://www.ilo.org/public/english/standard/relm/itc/ilc 95/pdf/rep-i-b.pdf p.67> accessed on 16th May, 2013.
[20] *Ibid.*

about *Child Rights* especially involving those NGOs who have been active in working with children and protecting their rights.[21]

There is a need to accelerate training and capacity building for, realization of *Child Rights*, government servants at all levels, in all departments, especially Social Welfare, Health Education, Labour and Staff of other agencies working with children should be trained in *Child Rights*. Training and sensitization of police personnel and all enforcement staff is a priority. All field-level functionaries of various departments who provide services to children requires sensitization and orientation on child right as part of their basic and refresher training. Teachers and Health Workers should be prioritized for sensitization on *Child Rights*. Orientation and sensitization of Panchayat members and functionaries of local bodies on *Child Rights* is needed. CRC should be integrated into training curriculum of various institutions like NIPCCD, IAS Academy and IPS Academy, Local Bodies, State Academies of Administration and other major National and State Level Training Institutions. Existing training and rights related knowledge base of civil society needs to be institutionalized as a resource base for the country for accelerating CRC implementation parents, community members, media personnel, NGOs and other agencies working for children require special training on *Child Rights*.[22]

Lack of accountability, information and proper documentation hinders effective co-ordination and monitoring of child right at all levels. Urgent action is required to strengthen these aspects. It is also imperative to empower existing committees set up for children's programme to monitor *Child Rights* at State, District, block and village levels. It should be in consultation with and having representation from government civil society, NGOs, gram panchayats and children.[23]

---

[21] See *Supra* note 3.
[22] *Ibid*, pp.25-26.
[23] *Ibid*.

Each State should have a Co-ordination Committee to collect data on all aspects of *Child Rights*. Existing data collection systems needs to be reviewed, as there are many areas where adequate and disaggregated data are not available. This include gender disaggregated data, and information on various forms of child abuse and exploitation, child labour, children affected by conflict/militancy, trafficking of children, tribal and indigenous children and their conditions, crimes committed against children, conditions of children in State-run-institution etc.[24]

Children should be encouraged to express their views. They should also be given the opportunity and encouraged to learn and develop participatory and thinking skills, as well as skills of developing and articulating ideas. They should be provided the opportunity and the platform to present their views and suggestions, which should be received with respect and suitably considered. Children should be the partners in developing the strategy for implementation and monitoring of CRC in the country and reporting on violation of their rights.[25] Already the work is being done in this direction, the UN General Assembly special session on children was held in New York in 2002, the report published highlights 12 lessons learned in supporting children participation in UN General Assembly Special Session on Children.[26] Another remarkable step, is the creation of Bal Panchayat, with an objective to make children aware of their fundamental rights. In this direction CASP-Plan has launched a number of program that take into account the intellectual and emotional needs of children.[27] But still a lot is required to be done in this context.

Good parenting and child care education must be given to parents, teachers and staff of child care institutions. Families are the primary care providers for children

---

[24] *Ibid,* p.27.
[25] *Ibid.*
[26] <www.crin.org/docs/resouces/publications/12lessons_sc.pdf> accessed on 17th October, 2012.
[27] <www.balpanchayat.org/intoduction.htm> accessed on 17th October, 2006

and the capacity of families for care and protection of children has to be strengthened, especially of families in the most marginalized groups.[28]

Enacting the legislations drafting the policies and programme is not sufficient to deal with the various problems of violation relating to child. The legislation and policies have to be implemented and monitored regularly to achieve the desired objectives. In Krist Pereira case[29] and Prerana case[30] the High Court has given directions to form committees for the recommendation to the State Government for proper functioning of Juvenile Justice System and supervise the rehabilitation of rescued girls respectively. This can be the one method of effective implementation of laws. Another is appointment of ombudsperson for children as such an ombudsman first appeared in the early 1980s in Sweden and Norway. In order to be really the voice of children, the ombudsperson must be an independent body and be able to express freely his or her opinion on action undertaken by public administration reprimanding where necessary the lack of a system. The ombudsperson should able to promote authoritatively the best interest of children.[31]

In brief the need is to mould attitude and perception of adults and children towards *Child Rights*. For this, each one of us as an important member of civilized society must fulfill our obligation to the young generation by providing, conducive environment to every child so that it's all round personality, physical, mental, moral and spiritual is developed. Especially, in relation to children from the weaker section of the society, an effective safety net must be created in order to protect them from not being devoured by the powerful crime mafia of the society. In India, already much work has been done by the government in this direction yet there is lot more to be done in practice for proper enforcement of their rights and effective implementation of laws, policies and programmes relating to survival and welfare of

---

[28] *Ibid*, p.30.
[29] *Krist Pereira v. State of Maharastra*. Criminal Writ Petition No.1107 of 1996, Mumbai High Court. The Court directed to constitute a permanent body called Maharastra State Monitoring Committee.
[30] *Perana v. State of Mahrastra* Criminal Writ Petition No.1332 of 1999. Mumbai High Court. The Hon'ble Court constituted a Monitoring and Guidance Committee to supervise the functioning of the rehabilitation Home and ensure proper rehabilitation of the rescued girls.
[31] See *Supra* note 6, p.475.

children. Let us work together to provide fear free, peaceful world to our future generations especially the poor ones so that they should not feel deprived from the feel of what real childhood is. As rightly observed by Kofi A. Annan, the Secretary General of the UN that *"There is no trust more sacred than the one the world holds with children, there is no duty more important than ensuring their rights are respected and their welfare is protected…..* *"[32]*

[32] Foreword by Kofi A. Annan in 'The State of World's Children, 2000', quoted in Mamta Rao, *Law Relating to Women and Children*, (Eastern Book Company, 2005), pp. 444-445.

ANNEXURE I

CONVENTION ON THE RIGHTS OF THE CHILD

Adopted and opened for signature, ratification and accession by General Assembly resolution 44/25 of 20 November 1989 *entry into force* **2 September 1990, in accordance with article 49**

Preamble

The States Parties to the present Convention,

Considering that, in accordance with the principles proclaimed in the Charter of the United Nations, recognition of the inherent dignity and of the equal and inalienable rights of all members of the human family is the foundation of freedom, justice and peace in t

he world,

Bearing in mind that the peoples of the United Nations have, in the Charter, reaffirmed their faith in fundamental human rights and in the dignity and worth of the human person, and have determined to promote social progress and better standards of life in larger freedom,

Recognizing that the United Nations has, in the Universal Declaration of Human Rights and in the International Covenants on Human Rights, proclaimed and agreed that everyone is entitled to all the rights and freedoms set forth therein, without distinction of any kind, such as race, colour, sex, language, religion, political or other opinion, national or social origin, property, birth or other status,

Recalling that, in the Universal Declaration of Human Rights, the United Nations has proclaimed that childhood is entitled to special care and assistance,

Convinced that the family, as the fundamental group of society and the natural environment for the growth and well-being of all its members and particularly children, should be afforded the necessary protection and assistance so that it can fully assume its responsibilities within the community,

Recognizing that the child, for the full and harmonious development of his or her personality, should grow up in a family environment, in an atmosphere of happiness, love and understanding,

Considering that the child should be fully prepared to live an individual life in society, and brought up in the spirit of the ideals proclaimed in the Charter of the United Nations, and in particular in the spirit of peace, dignity, tolerance, freedom, equality and solidarity,

Bearing in mind that the need to extend particular care to the child has been stated in the Geneva Declaration of the Rights of the Child of 1924 and in the Declaration of the Rights of the Child adopted by the General Assembly on 20 November 1959 and recognized in the Universal Declaration of Human Rights, in the International Covenant on Civil and Political Rights (in particular in articles 23 and 24), in the International Covenant on Economic, Social and Cultural Rights (in particular in article 10) and in the statutes and relevant instruments of specialized agencies and international organizations concerned with the welfare of children, '

Bearing in mind that, as indicated in the Declaration of the Rights of the Child, "the child, by reason of his physical and mental immaturity, needs special safeguards and care, including appropriate legal protection, before as well as after birth",

Recalling the provisions of the Declaration on Social and Legal Principles relating to the Protection and Welfare of Children, with Special Reference to Foster Placement and Adoption Nationally and Internationally; the United Nations Standard Minimum Rules for the Administration of Juvenile Justice (The Beijing Rules) ; and the Declaration on the Protection of Women and Children in Emergency and Armed Conflict,

Recognizing that, in all countries in the world, there are children living in exceptionally difficult conditions, and that such children need special consideration,

Taking due account of the importance of the traditions and cultural values of each people for the protection and harmonious development of the child,

Recognizing the importance of international co-operation for improving the living conditions of children in every country, in particular in the developing countries,

Have agreed as follows:

PART I

Article 1

For the purposes of the present Convention, a child means every human being below the age of eighteen years unless under the law applicable to the child, majority is attained earlier.

Article 2

1. States Parties shall respect and ensure the rights set forth in the present Convention to each child within their jurisdiction without discrimination of any kind, irrespective of the child's or his or her parent's or legal guardian's race, colour, sex, language, religion, political or other opinion, national, ethnic or social origin, property, disability, birth or other status.

2. States Parties shall take all appropriate measures to ensure that the child is protected against all forms of discrimination or punishment on the basis of the status, activities, expressed opinions, or beliefs of the child's parents, legal guardians, or family members.

Article 3

1. In all actions concerning children, whether undertaken by public or private social welfare institutions, courts of law, administrative authorities or legislative bodies, the best interests of the child shall be a primary consideration.

2. States Parties undertake to ensure the child such protection and care as is necessary for his or her well-being, taking into account the rights and duties of his or her parents, legal guardians, or other individuals legally responsible for him or her, and, to this end, shall take all appropriate legislative and administrative measures.

3. States Parties shall ensure that the institutions, services and facilities responsible for the care or protection of children shall conform with the standards established by competent authorities, particularly in the areas of safety, health, in the number and suitability of their staff, as well as competent supervision.

Article 4

States Parties shall undertake all appropriate legislative, administrative, and other measures for the implementation of the rights recognized in the present Convention. With regard to economic, social and cultural rights, States Parties shall undertake such measures to the maximum extent of their available resources and, where needed, within the framework of international co-operation.

Article 5

States Parties shall respect the responsibilities, rights and duties of parents or, where applicable, the members of the extended family or community as provided for by local custom, legal guardians or other persons legally responsible for the child, to provide, in a manner consistent with the evolving capacities of the child, appropriate direction and guidance in the exercise by the child of the rights recognized in the present Convention.

Article 6

1. States Parties recognize that every child has the inherent right to life.

2. States Parties shall ensure to the maximum extent possible the survival and development of the child.

Article 7

1. The child shall be registered immediately after birth and shall have the right from birth to a name, the right to acquire a nationality and. as far as possible, the right to know and be cared for by his or her parents.

2. States Parties shall ensure the implementation of these rights in accordance with their national law and their obligations under the relevant international instruments in this field, in particular where the child would otherwise be stateless.

Article 8

1. States Parties undertake to respect the right of the child to preserve his or her identity, including nationality, name and family relations as recognized by law without unlawful interference.

2. Where a child is illegally deprived of some or all of the elements of his or her identity, States Parties shall provide appropriate assistance and protection, with a view to re-establishing speedily his or her identity.

Article 9

1. States Parties shall ensure that a child shall not be separated from his or her parents against their will, except when competent authorities subject to judicial review determine, in accordance with applicable law and procedures, that such separation is necessary for the best interests of the child. Such determination may be necessary in a particular case such as one involving abuse or neglect of the child by the parents, or one where the parents are living separately and a decision must be made as to the child's place of residence.

2. In any proceedings pursuant to paragraph 1 of the present article, all interested parties shall be given an opportunity to participate in the proceedings and make their views known.

3. States Parties shall respect the right of the child who is separated from one or both parents to maintain personal relations and direct contact with both parents on a regular basis, except if it is contrary to the child's best interests. 4. Where such separation results from any action initiated by a State Party, such as the detention, imprisonment, exile, deportation or death (including death arising from any cause while the person is in the custody of the State) of one or both parents or of the child, that State Party shall, upon request, provide the parents, the child or, if appropriate, another member of the family with the essential information concerning the whereabouts of the absent member(s) of the family unless the provision of the information would be detrimental to the well-being of the child. States Parties shall further ensure that the submission of such a request shall of itself entail no adverse consequences for the person(s) concerned.

Article 10

1. In accordance with the obligation of States Parties under article 9, paragraph 1, applications by a child or his or her parents to enter or leave a State Party for the purpose of family reunification shall be dealt with by States Parties in a positive, humane and expeditious manner. States Parties shall further ensure that the submission of such a request shall entail no adverse consequences for the applicants and for the members of their family.

2. A child whose parents reside in different States shall have the right to maintain on a regular basis, save in exceptional circumstances personal relations and direct contacts with both parents. Towards that end and in accordance with the obligation of States Parties under article 9, paragraph 1, States Parties shall respect the right of the child and his or her parents to leave any country, including their own, and to enter their own country. The right to leave any country shall be subject only to such

restrictions as are prescribed by law and which are necessary to protect the national security, public order (order public), public health or morals or the rights and freedoms of others and are consistent with the other rights recognized in the present Convention.

Article 11

1. States Parties shall take measures to combat the illicit transfer and non-return of children abroad.

2. To this end, States Parties shall promote the conclusion of bilateral or multilateral agreements or accession to existing agreements.

Article 12

1. States Parties shall assure to the child who is capable of forming his or her own views the right to express those views freely in all matters affecting the child, the views of the child being given due weight in accordance with the age and maturity of the child.

2. For this purpose, the child shall in particular be provided the opportunity to be heard in any judicial and administrative proceedings affecting the child, either directly, or through a representative or an appropriate body, in a manner consistent with the procedural rules of national law.

Article 13

1. The child shall have the right to freedom of expression; this right shall include freedom to seek, receive and impart information and ideas of all kinds, regardless of frontiers, either orally, in writing or in print, in the form of art, or through any other media of the child's choice.

2. The exercise of this right may be subject to certain restrictions, but these shall only be such as are provided by law and are necessary:

(a) For respect of the rights or reputations of others; or

(b) For the protection of national security or of public order (ordre public), or of public health or morals.

Article 14

1. States Parties shall respect the right of the child to freedom of thought, conscience and religion.

2. States Parties shall respect the rights and duties of the parents and, when applicable, legal guardians, to provide direction to the child in the exercise of his or her right in a manner consistent with the evolving capacities of the child.

3. Freedom to manifest one's religion or beliefs may be subject only to such limitations as are prescribed by law and are necessary to protect public safety, order, health or morals, or the fundamental rights and freedoms of others.

Article 15

1. States Parties recognize the rights of the child to freedom of association and to freedom of peaceful assembly.

2. No restrictions may be placed on the exercise of these rights other than those imposed in conformity with the law and which are necessary in a democratic society in the interests of national security or public safety, public order (order public), the protection of public health or morals or the protection of the rights and freedoms of others.

Article 16

1. No child shall be subjected to arbitrary or unlawful interference with his or her privacy, family, home or correspondence, nor to unlawful attacks on his or her honour and reputation.

2. The child has the right to the protection of the law against such interference or attacks.

Article 17

States Parties recognize the important function performed by the mass media and shall ensure that the child has access to information and material from a diversity of national and international sources, especially those aimed at the promotion of his or her social, spiritual and moral well-being and physical and mental health. To this end, States Parties shall:

(a) Encourage the mass media to disseminate information and material of social and cultural benefit to the child and in accordance with the spirit of article 29;

(b) Encourage international co-operation in the production, exchange and dissemination of such information and material from a diversity of cultural, national and international sources;

(c) Encourage the production and dissemination of children's books;

(d) Encourage the mass media to have particular regard to the linguistic needs of the child who belongs to a minority group or who is indigenous;

(e) Encourage the development of appropriate guidelines for the protection of the child from information and material injurious to his or her well-being, bearing in mind the provisions of articles 13 and 18.

Article 18

1. States Parties shall use their best efforts to ensure recognition of the principle that both parents have common responsibilities for the upbringing and development of the child. Parents or, as the case may be, legal guardians, have the primary responsibility for the upbringing and development of the child. The best interests of the child will be their basic concern.

2. For the purpose of guaranteeing and promoting the rights set forth in the present Convention, States Parties shall render appropriate assistance to parents and legal

guardians in the performance of their child-rearing responsibilities and shall ensure the development of institutions, facilities and services for the care of children.

3. States Parties shall take all appropriate measures to ensure that children of working parents have the right to benefit from child-care services and facilities for which they are eligible.

Article 19

1. States Parties shall take all appropriate legislative, administrative, social and educational measures to protect the child from all forms of physical or mental violence, injury or abuse, neglect or negligent treatment, maltreatment or exploitation, including sexual abuse, while in the care of parent(s), legal guardian(s) or any other person who has the care of the child.

2. Such protective measures should, as appropriate, include effective procedures for the establishment of social programmes to provide necessary support for the child and for those who have the care of the child, as well as for other forms of prevention and for identification, reporting, referral, investigation, treatment and follow-up of instances of child maltreatment described heretofore, and, as appropriate, for judicial involvement.

Article 20

1. A child temporarily or permanently deprived of his or her family environment, or in whose own best interests cannot be allowed to remain in that environment, shall be entitled to special protection and assistance provided by the State.

2. States Parties shall in accordance with their national laws ensure alternative care for such a child.

3. Such care could include, inter alia, foster placement, kafalah of Islamic law, adoption or if necessary placement in suitable institutions for the care of children. When considering solutions, due regard shall be paid to the desirability of continuity

in a child's upbringing and to the child's ethnic, religious, cultural and linguistic background.

Article 21

States Parties that recognize and/or permit the system of adoption shall ensure that the best interests of the child shall be the paramount consideration and they shall:

(a) Ensure that the adoption of a child is authorized only by competent authorities who determine, in accordance with applicable law and procedures and on the basis of all pertinent and reliable information, that the adoption is permissible in view of the child's status concerning parents, relatives and legal guardians and that, if required, the persons concerned have given their informed consent to the adoption on the basis of such counselling as may be necessary;

(b) Recognize that inter-country adoption may be considered as an alternative means of child's care, if the child cannot be placed in a foster or an adoptive family or cannot in any suitable manner be cared for in the child's country of origin; (c) Ensure that the child concerned by inter-country adoption enjoys safeguards and standards equivalent to those existing in the case of national adoption;

(d) Take all appropriate measures to ensure that, in inter-country adoption, the placement does not result in improper financial gain for those involved in it;

(e) Promote, where appropriate, the objectives of the present article by concluding bilateral or multilateral arrangements or agreements, and endeavour, within this framework, to ensure that the placement of the child in another country is carried out by competent authorities or organs.

Article 22

1. States Parties shall take appropriate measures to ensure that a child who is seeking refugee status or who is considered a refugee in accordance with applicable international or domestic law and procedures shall, whether unaccompanied or

accompanied by his or her parents or by any other person, receive appropriate protection and humanitarian assistance in the enjoyment of applicable rights set forth in the present Convention and in other international human rights or humanitarian instruments to which the said States are Parties.

2. For this purpose, States Parties shall provide, as they consider appropriate, co-operation in any efforts by the United Nations and other competent intergovernmental organizations or non-governmental organizations co-operating with the United Nations to protect and assist such a child and to trace the parents or other members of the family of any refugee child in order to obtain information necessary for reunification with his or her family. In cases where no parents or other members of the family can be found, the child shall be accorded the same protection as any other child permanently or temporarily deprived of his or her family environment for any reason , as set forth in the present Convention.

Article 23

1. States Parties recognize that a mentally or physically disabled child should enjoy a full and decent life, in conditions which ensure dignity, promote self-reliance and facilitate the child's active participation in the community.

2. States Parties recognize the right of the disabled child to special care and shall encourage and ensure the extension, subject to available resources, to the eligible child and those responsible for his or her care, of assistance for which application is made and which is appropriate to the child's condition and to the circumstances of the parents or others caring for the child. 3. Recognizing the special needs of a disabled child, assistance extended in accordance with paragraph 2 of the present article shall be provided free of charge, whenever possible, taking into account the financial resources of the parents or others caring for the child, and shall be designed to ensure that the disabled child has effective access to and receives education, training, health care services, rehabilitation services, preparation for employment and recreation opportunities in a manner conducive to the child's achieving the fullest possible social

integration and individual development, including his or her cultural and spiritual development

4. States Parties shall promote, in the spirit of international cooperation, the exchange of appropriate information in the field of preventive health care and of medical, psychological and functional treatment of disabled children, including dissemination of and access to information concerning methods of rehabilitation, education and vocational services, with the aim of enabling States Parties to improve their capabilities and skills and to widen their experience in these areas. In this regard, particular account shall be taken of the needs of developing countries.

Article 24

1. States Parties recognize the right of the child to the enjoyment of the highest attainable standard of health and to facilities for the treatment of illness and rehabilitation of health. States Parties shall strive to ensure that no child is deprived of his or her right of access to such health care services.

2. States Parties shall pursue full implementation of this right and, in particular, shall take appropriate measures:

(a) To diminish infant and child mortality;

(b) To ensure the provision of necessary medical assistance and health care to all children with emphasis on the development of primary health care;

(c) To combat disease and malnutrition, including within the framework of primary health care, through, inter alia, the application of readily available technology and through the provision of adequate nutritious foods and clean drinking-water, taking into consideration the dangers and risks of environmental pollution;

(d) To ensure appropriate pre-natal and post-natal health care for mothers;

(e) To ensure that all segments of society, in particular parents and children, are informed, have access to education and are supported in the use of basic knowledge of child health and nutrition, the advantages of breastfeeding, hygiene and environmental sanitation and the prevention of accidents;

(f) To develop preventive health care, guidance for parents and family planning education and services.

3. States Parties shall take all effective and appropriate measures with a view to abolishing traditional practices prejudicial to the health of children.

4. States Parties undertake to promote and encourage international co-operation with a view to achieving progressively the full realization of the right recognized in the present article. In this regard, particular account shall be taken of the needs of developing countries.

Article 25

States Parties recognize the right of a child who has been placed by the competent authorities for the purposes of care, protection or treatment of his or her physical or mental health, to a periodic review of the treatment provided to the child and all other circumstances relevant to his or her placement.

Article 26

1. States Parties shall recognize for every child the right to benefit from social security, including social insurance, and shall take the necessary measures to achieve the full realization of this right in accordance with their national law.

2. The benefits should, where appropriate, be granted, taking into account the resources and the circumstances of the child and persons having responsibility for the maintenance of the child, as well as any other consideration relevant to an application for benefits made by or on behalf of the child.

Article 27

1. States Parties recognize the right of every child to a standard of living adequate for the child's physical, mental, spiritual, moral and social development.

2. The parent(s) or others responsible for the child have the primary responsibility to secure, within their abilities and financial capacities, the conditions of living necessary for the child's development.

3. States Parties, in accordance with national conditions and within their means, shall take appropriate measures to assist parents and others responsible for the child to implement this right and shall in case of need provide material assistance and support programmes, particularly with regard to nutrition, clothing and housing.

4. States Parties shall take all appropriate measures to secure the recovery of maintenance for the child from the parents or other persons having financial responsibility for the child, both within the State Party and from abroad. In particular, where the person having financial responsibility for the child lives in a State different from that of the child, States Parties shall promote the accession to international agreements or the conclusion of such agreements, as well as the making of other appropriate arrangements.

Article 28

1. States Parties recognize the right of the child to education, and with a view to achieving this right progressively and on the basis of equal opportunity, they shall, in particular:

(a) Make primary education compulsory and available free to all;

(b) Encourage the development of different forms of secondary education, including general and vocational education, make them available and accessible to every child, and take appropriate measures such as the introduction of free education and offering financial assistance in case of need;

(c) Make higher education accessible to all on the basis of capacity by every appropriate means;

(d) Make educational and vocational information and guidance available and accessible to all children;

(e) Take measures to encourage regular attendance at schools and the reduction of drop-out rates.

2. States Parties shall take all appropriate measures to ensure that school discipline is administered in a manner consistent with the child's human dignity and in conformity with the present Convention.

3. States Parties shall promote and encourage international cooperation in matters relating to education, in particular with a view to contributing to the elimination of ignorance and illiteracy throughout the world and facilitating access to scientific and technical knowledge and modern teaching methods. In this regard, particular account shall be taken of the needs of developing countries.

Article 29

1. States Parties agree that the education of the child shall be directed to:

(a) The development of the child's personality, talents and mental and physical abilities to their fullest potential;

(b) The development of respect for human rights and fundamental freedoms, and for the principles enshrined in the Charter of the United Nations;

(c) The development of respect for the child's parents, his or her own cultural identity, language and values, for the national values of the country in which the child is living, the country from which he or she may originate, and for civilizations different from his or her own;

(d) The preparation of the child for responsible life in a free society, in the spirit of understanding, peace, tolerance, equality of sexes, and friendship among all peoples, ethnic, national and religious groups and persons of indigenous origin;

(e) The development of respect for the natural environment.

2. No part of the present article or article 28 shall be construed so as to interfere with the liberty of individuals and bodies to establish and direct educational institutions, subject always to the observance of the principle set forth in paragraph 1 of the present article and to the requirements that the education given in such institutions shall conform to such minimum standards as may be laid down by the State.

Article 30

In those States in which ethnic, religious or linguistic minorities or persons of indigenous origin exist, a child belonging to such a minority or who is indigenous shall not be denied the right, in community with other members of his or her group, to enjoy his or her own culture, to profess and practise his or her own religion, or to use his or her own language.

Article 31

1. States Parties recognize the right of the child to rest and leisure, to engage in play and recreational activities appropriate to the age of the child and to participate freely in cultural life and the arts.

2. States Parties shall respect and promote the right of the child to participate fully in cultural and artistic life and shall encourage the provision of appropriate and equal opportunities for cultural, artistic, recreational and leisure activity.

Article 32

1. States Parties recognize the right of the child to be protected from economic exploitation and from performing any work that is likely to be hazardous or to

interfere with the child's education, or to be harmful to the child's health or physical, mental, spiritual, moral or social development.

2. States Parties shall take legislative, administrative, social and educational measures to ensure the implementation of the present article. To this end, and having regard to the relevant provisions of other international instruments, States Parties shall in particular: (a) Provide for a minimum age or minimum ages for admission to employment;

(b) Provide for appropriate regulation of the hours and conditions of employment;

(c) Provide for appropriate penalties or other sanctions to ensure the effective enforcement of the present article.

Article 33

States Parties shall take all appropriate measures, including legislative, administrative, social and educational measures, to protect children from the illicit use of narcotic drugs and psychotropic substances as defined in the relevant international treaties, and to prevent the use of children in the illicit production and trafficking of such substances.

Article 34

States Parties undertake to protect the child from all forms of sexual exploitation and sexual abuse. For these purposes, States Parties shall in particular take all appropriate national, bilateral and multilateral measures to prevent:

(a) The inducement or coercion of a child to engage in any unlawful sexual activity;

(b) The exploitative use of children in prostitution or other unlawful sexual practices;

(c) The exploitative use of children in pornographic performances and materials.

Article 35

States Parties shall take all appropriate national, bilateral and multilateral measures to prevent the abduction of, the sale of or traffic in children for any purpose or in any form.

Article 36

States Parties shall protect the child against all other forms of exploitation prejudicial to any aspects of the child's welfare.

Article 37

States Parties shall ensure that:

(a) No child shall be subjected to torture or other cruel, inhuman or degrading treatment or punishment. Neither capital punishment nor life imprisonment without possibility of release shall be imposed for offences committed by persons below eighteen years of age;

(b) No child shall be deprived of his or her liberty unlawfully or arbitrarily. The arrest, detention or imprisonment of a child shall be in conformity with the law and shall be used only as a measure of last resort and for the shortest appropriate period of time;

(c) Every child deprived of liberty shall be treated with humanity and respect for the inherent dignity of the human person, and in a manner which takes into account the needs of persons of his or her age. In particular, every child deprived of liberty shall be separated from adults unless it is considered in the child's best interest not to do so and shall have the right to maintain contact with his or her family through correspondence and visits, save in exceptional circumstances;

(d) Every child deprived of his or her liberty shall have the right to prompt access to legal and other appropriate assistance, as well as the right to challenge the legality of the deprivation of his or her liberty before a court or other competent, independent and impartial authority, and to a prompt decision on any such action.

Article 38

1. States Parties undertake to respect and to ensure respect for rules of international humanitarian law applicable to them in armed conflicts which are relevant to the child.

2. States Parties shall take all feasible measures to ensure that persons who have not attained the age of fifteen years do not take a direct part in hostilities.

3. States Parties shall refrain from recruiting any person who has not attained the age of fifteen years into their armed forces. In recruiting among those persons who have attained the age of fifteen years but who have not attained the age of eighteen years, States Parties shall endeavor to give priority to those who are oldest.

4. In accordance with their obligations under international humanitarian law to protect the civilian population in armed conflicts, States Parties shall take all feasible measures to ensure protection and care of children who are affected by an armed conflict.

Article 39

States Parties shall take all appropriate measures to promote physical and psychological recovery and social reintegration of a child victim of: any form of neglect, exploitation, or abuse; torture or any other form of cruel, inhuman or degrading treatment or punishment; or armed conflicts. Such recovery and reintegration shall take place in an environment which fosters the health, self-respect and dignity of the child.

Article 40

1. States Parties recognize the right of every child alleged as, accused of, or recognized as having infringed the penal law to be treated in a manner consistent with

the promotion of the child's sense of dignity and worth, which reinforces the child's respect for the human rights and fundamental freedoms of others and which takes into account the child's age and the desirability of promoting the child's reintegration and the child's assuming a constructive role in society.

2. To this end, and having regard to the relevant provisions of international instruments, States Parties shall, in particular, ensure that:

(a) No child shall be alleged as, be accused of, or recognized as having infringed the penal law by reason of acts or omissions that were not prohibited by national or international law at the time they were committed;

(b) Every child alleged as or accused of having infringed the penal law has at least the following guarantees:

(i) To be presumed innocent until proven guilty according to law;

(ii) To be informed promptly and directly of the charges against him or her, and, if appropriate, through his or her parents or legal guardians, and to have legal or other appropriate assistance in the preparation and presentation of his or her defence;

(iii) To have the matter determined without delay by a competent, independent and impartial authority or judicial body in a fair hearing according to law, in the presence of legal or other appropriate assistance and, unless it is considered not to be in the best interest of the child, in particular, taking into account his or her age or situation, his or her parents or legal guardians;

(iv) Not to be compelled to give testimony or to confess guilt; to examine or have examined adverse witnesses and to obtain the participation and examination of witnesses on his or her behalf under conditions of equality;

(v) If considered to have infringed the penal law, to have this decision and any measures imposed in consequence thereof reviewed by a higher competent, independent and impartial authority or judicial body according to law;

(vi) To have the free assistance of an interpreter if the child cannot understand or speak the language used;

(vii) To have his or her privacy fully respected at all stages of the proceedings. 3. States Parties shall seek to promote the establishment of laws, procedures, authorities and institutions specifically applicable to children alleged as, accused of, or recognized as having infringed the penal law, and, in particular:

(a) The establishment of a minimum age below which children shall be presumed not to have the capacity to infringe the penal law;

(b) Whenever appropriate and desirable, measures for dealing with such children without resorting to judicial proceedings, providing that human rights and legal safeguards are fully respected.

4. A variety of dispositions, such as care, guidance and supervision orders; counselling; probation; foster care; education and vocational training programmes and other alternatives to institutional care shall be available to ensure that children are dealt with in a manner appropriate to their well-being and proportionate both to their circumstances and the offence.

Article 41

Nothing in the present Convention shall affect any provisions which are more conducive to the realization of the rights of the child and which may be contained in:

(a) The law of a State party; or

(b) International law in force for that State.

PART II

Article 42

States Parties undertake to make the principles and provisions of the Convention widely known, by appropriate and active means, to adults and children alike.

Article 43

1. For the purpose of examining the progress made by States Parties in achieving the realization of the obligations undertaken in the present Convention, there shall be established a <u>Committee on the Rights of the Child</u>, which shall carry out the functions hereinafter provided.

2. The Committee shall consist of ten experts of high moral standing and recognized competence in the field covered by this Convention. The members of the Committee shall be elected by States Parties from among their nationals and shall serve in their personal capacity, consideration being given to equitable geographical distribution, as well as to the principal legal systems.

3. The members of the Committee shall be elected by secret ballot from a list of persons nominated by States Parties. Each State Party may nominate one person from among its own nationals.

4. The initial election to the Committee shall be held no later than six months after the date of the entry into force of the present Convention and thereafter every second year. At least four months before the date of each election, the Secretary-General of the United Nations shall address a letter to States Parties inviting them to submit their nominations within two months. The Secretary-General shall subsequently prepare a list in alphabetical order of all persons thus nominated, indicating States Parties which have nominated them, and shall submit it to the States Parties to the present Convention.

5. The elections shall be held at meetings of States Parties convened by the Secretary-General at United Nations Headquarters. At those meetings, for which two thirds of States Parties shall constitute a quorum, the persons elected to the Committee shall be those who obtain the largest number of votes and an absolute majority of the votes of the representatives of States Parties present and voting.

6. The members of the Committee shall be elected for a term of four years. They shall be eligible for re-election if renominated. The term of five of the members elected at the first election shall expire at the end of two years; immediately after the first election, the names of these five members shall be chosen by lot by the Chairman of the meeting.

7. If a member of the Committee dies or resigns or declares that for any other cause he or she can no longer perform the duties of the Committee, the State Party which nominated the member shall appoint another expert from among its nationals to serve for the remainder of the term, subject to the approval of the Committee.

8. The Committee shall establish its own rules of procedure.

9. The Committee shall elect its officers for a period of two years.

10. The meetings of the Committee shall normally be held at United Nations Headquarters or at any other convenient place as determined by the Committee. The Committee shall normally meet annually. The duration of the meetings of the Committee shall be determined, and reviewed, if necessary, by a meeting of the States Parties to the present Convention, subject to the approval of the General Assembly.

11. The Secretary-General of the United Nations shall provide the necessary staff and facilities for the effective performance of the functions of the Committee under the present Convention.

12. With the approval of the General Assembly, the members of the Committee established under the present Convention shall receive emoluments from United Nations resources on such terms and conditions as the Assembly may decide.

Article 44

1. States Parties undertake to submit to the Committee, through the Secretary-General of the United Nations, reports on the measures they have adopted which give effect to the rights recognized herein and on the progress made on the enjoyment of those rights:

(a) Within two years of the entry into force of the Convention for the State Party concerned;

(b) Thereafter every five years.

2. Reports made under the present article shall indicate factors and difficulties, if any, affecting the degree of fulfilment of the obligations under the present Convention. Reports shall also contain sufficient information to provide the Committee with a comprehensive understanding of the implementation of the Convention in the country concerned.

3. A State Party which has submitted a comprehensive initial report to the Committee need not, in its subsequent reports submitted in accordance with paragraph 1 (b) of the present article, repeat basic information previously provided.

4. The Committee may request from States Parties further information relevant to the implementation of the Convention.

5. The Committee shall submit to the General Assembly, through the Economic and Social Council, every two years, reports on its activities.

6. States Parties shall make their reports widely available to the public in their own countries.

Article 45

In order to foster the effective implementation of the Convention and to encourage international co-operation in the field covered by the Convention:

(a) The specialized agencies, the United Nations Children's Fund, and other United Nations organs shall be entitled to be represented at the consideration of the implementation of such provisions of the present Convention as fall within the scope of their mandate. The Committee may invite the specialized agencies, the United Nations Children's Fund and other competent bodies as it may consider appropriate to provide expert advice on the implementation of the Convention in areas falling within the scope of their respective mandates. The Committee may invite the specialized agencies, the United Nations Children's Fund, and other United Nations organs to submit reports on the implementation of the Convention in areas falling within the scope of their activities;

(b) The Committee shall transmit, as it may consider appropriate, to the specialized agencies, the United Nations Children's Fund and other competent bodies, any reports from States Parties that contain a request, or indicate a need, for technical advice or assistance, along with the Committee's observations and suggestions, if any, on these requests or indications;

(c) The Committee may recommend to the General Assembly to request the Secretary-General to undertake on its behalf studies on specific issues relating to the rights of the child;

(d) The Committee may make suggestions and general recommendations based on information received pursuant to articles 44 and 45 of the present Convention. Such suggestions and general recommendations shall be transmitted to any State Party concerned and reported to the General Assembly, together with comments, if any, from States Parties.

PART III

Article 46

The present Convention shall be open for signature by all States.

Article 47

The present Convention is subject to ratification. Instruments of ratification shall be deposited with the Secretary-General of the United Nations.

Article 48

The present Convention shall remain open for accession by any State. The instruments of accession shall be deposited with the Secretary-General of the United Nations.

Article 49

1. The present Convention shall enter into force on the thirtieth day following the date of deposit with the Secretary-General of the United Nations of the twentieth instrument of ratification or accession.

2. For each State ratifying or acceding to the Convention after the deposit of the twentieth instrument of ratification or accession, the Convention shall enter into force on the thirtieth day after the deposit by such State of its instrument of ratification or accession.

Article 50

1. Any State Party may propose an amendment and file it with the Secretary-General of the United Nations. The Secretary-General shall thereupon communicate the proposed amendment to States Parties, with a request that they indicate whether they favour a conference of States Parties for the purpose of considering and voting upon the proposals. In the event that, within four months from the date of such communication, at least one third of the States Parties favour such a conference, the Secretary-General shall convene the conference under the auspices of the United

Nations. Any amendment adopted by a majority of States Parties present and voting at the conference shall be submitted to the General Assembly for approval.

2. An amendment adopted in accordance with paragraph 1 of the present article shall enter into force when it has been approved by the General Assembly of the United Nations and accepted by a two-thirds majority of States Parties.

3. When an amendment enters into force, it shall be binding on those States Parties which have accepted it, other States Parties still being bound by the provisions of the present Convention and any earlier amendments which they have accepted.

Article 51

1. The Secretary-General of the United Nations shall receive and circulate to all States the text of reservations made by States at the time of ratification or accession.

2. A reservation incompatible with the object and purpose of the present Convention shall not be permitted.

3. Reservations may be withdrawn at any time by notification to that effect addressed to the Secretary-General of the United Nations, who shall then inform all States. Such notification shall take effect on the date on which it is received by the Secretary-General

Article 52

A State Party may denounce the present Convention by written notification to the Secretary-General of the United Nations. Denunciation becomes effective one year after the date of receipt of the notification by the Secretary-General.

Article 53

The Secretary-General of the United Nations is designated as the depositary of the present Convention.

Article 54

The original of the present Convention, of which the Arabic, Chinese, English, French, Russian and Spanish texts are equally authentic, shall be deposited with the Secretary-General of the United Nations.

IN WITNESS THEREOF the undersigned plenipotentiaries, being duly authorized thereto by their respective governments, have signed the present Convention.

ANNEXURE II

CHILD LABOR (PROHIBITION AND REGULATION) ACT, 1986

PREAMBLE

[61 of 1986]

An Act to prohibit the engagement of children in certain employments and to regulate the conditions of work of children in certain other employments Be it enacted by Parliament in the Thirty-seventh Year of the Republic of India as follows:

PART I - PRELIMINARY

1. Short title, extent and commencement- (1) This Act may be called the Child Labour (Prohibition and Regulation) Act, 1986.

(2) It extends to the whole of India.

(3) The provisions of this Act, other than Part III, shall come into force at once, and Part III shall come into force on such date as the Central Government may, by notification in the Official Gazette, appoint, and different dates may be appointed for different States and for different classes of establishments.

2.Definitions.- In this Act, unless the context otherwise requires,-

(i) appropriate Government means, in relation to an establishment under the control of the Central Government or a railway administration or a major port or a mine or oilfield, the Central Government, and in all other cases, the State Government;

(ii) child means a person who has not completed his fourteenth year of age;

(iii) day means a period of twenty-four hours beginning at mid-night;

(iv) establishment includes a shop, commercial establishment, workshop, farm, residential hotel, restaurant, eating house, theatre or other place of public amusement or entertainment;

(v) family, in relation to an occupier, means the individual, the wife or husband, as the case may be, of such individual, and their children, brother or sister of such individual,

(vi) occupier, in relation to an establishment or a workshop, means the person who has the ultimate control over the affairs of the establishment or workshop;

(vii) port authority means any authority administering a port;

(viii) prescribed means prescribed by rules made under section 18;

(ix) week means a period of seven days beginning at midnight on Saturday night or such other night as may be approved in writing for a particular area by the Inspector;

(x) workshop means any premises (including the precincts thereof) wherein any industrial process is carried on, but does not include any premises to which the provisions of section 67 of the Factories Act, 1948(63 of 1948), for the time being, apply.

PART II PROHIBITION OF EMPLOYMENT OF CHILDREN IN CERTAIN OCCUPATIONS AND PROCESSES

3.Prohibition of employment of children in certain occupations and processes.- No child shall be employed or permitted to work in any of the occupations set forth in Part A of the Schedule or in any workshop wherein any of the processes set forth in Part B of the Schedule is carried on:

Provided that nothing in this section shall apply to any workshop wherein any process is carried on by the occupier with the aid of his family or to any school established by, or receiving assistance or recognition from, Government.

4. Power to amend the Schedule.- The Central Government, after giving by notification in the Official Gazette, not less than three months notice of its intention so to do, may, by like notification, add any occupation or process to the Schedule and thereupon the Schedule shall be deemed to have been amended accordingly.

5. Child Labour Technical Advisory Committee.- (1) The Central Government may, by notification in the Official Gazette, constitute an advisory committee to be called the Child Labour Technical Advisory Committee (hereafter in this section referred to as the Committee) to advise the Central Government for the purpose of addition of occupations and processes to the Schedule.

(2) The Committee shall consist of a Chairman and such other members not exceeding ten, as may be appointed by the Central Government.

(3) The Committee shall meet as often as it may consider necessary and shall have power to regulate its own procedure.

(4) The Committee may, if it deems it necessary so to do, constitute one or more sub-committees and may appoint to any such sub-committee, whether generally or for the consideration of any particular matter, any person who is not a member of the Committee.

(5) The term of office of, the manner of filling casual vacancies in the office of, and the allowances, if any, payable to, the Chairman and other members of the Committee, and the conditions and restrictions subject to which the Committee may appoint any person who is not a member of the Committee as a member of any of its sub-committees shall be such as may be prescribed.

PART III – REGULATION OF CONDITIONS OF WORK OF CHILDREN

6. Application of Part.- The provisions of this Part shall apply to an establishment or a class of establishment in which none of the occupations or processes referred to in section 3 is carried on.

7. Hours and period of work.- (1) No child shall be required or permitted to work in any establishment in excess of such number of hours as may prescribed for such establishment or class of establishments.

(2) The period of work on each day shall be so fixed that no period shall exceed three hours and that no child shall work for more than three hours before he has had an interval for rest for at least one hour.

(3) The period of work of a child shall b so arranged that inclusive of his interval for rest, under sub-section (2), it shall not be spread over more than six hours, including the time spent in waiting for work on any day.

(4) No child shall be permitted or required to work between 7 p.m.and 8 a.m.

(5) No child shall be permitted or required to work overtime.

(6) No child shall be required or permitted to work in any establishment on any day on which be has already been working in another establishment.

8. Weekly holidays.- Every child employed in an establishment shall be allowed in each week, a holiday of one whole day, which day shall be specified by the occupier in a notice permanently exhibited in a conspicuous place in the establishment and the day so specified shall not be altered by the occupier more than once in three months.

9. Notice to inspector.- (1) Every occupier in relation to an establishment in which a child was employed or permitted to work immediately before the date of commencement of this Act in relation to such establishment shall, within a period of thirty days from such commencement, send to the Inspector within whose local limits the establishment is situated, a written notice containing the following particular, s namely:-

(a) the name and situation of the establishment;

(b) the name of the person in actual management of the establishment;

(c) the address to which communications relating to the establishment should be sent; and

(d) the nature of the occupation or process carried on in the establishment.

(2) Every occupier, in relation to an establishment, who employs, or permits to work, any child after the date of commencement of this Act in relation to such establishment, shall, within a period of thirty days from the date of such employment, send to the Inspector within whose local limits the establishment is situated, a written notice containing the particulars as are mentioned in sub-section (1).

Explanation.-For the purposes of sub-sections (1) and (2), date of commencement of this Act, in relation to an establishment means the date of bringing into force of this Act in relation to such establishment.

(3) Nothing in sections 7, 8 and 9 shall apply to any establishment wherein any process is carried on by the occupier with the aid of his family or to any school established by, or receiving assistance or recognition from, Government.

10. Disputes as to age.- If any question arises between an Inspector and an occupier as to the age of any child who is employed or is permitted to work by him in an establishment, the question shall, in the absence of a certificate as to the age of such child granted by the prescribed medical authority, be referred by the Inspector for decision to the prescribed medical authority.

11.Maintenance of registar.- There shall be maintained by every occupier in respect of children employed or permitted to work in any establishment, a register to be available for inspection by an Inspector at all times during working hours or when work is being carried on in any such establishment, showing-

(a) the name and date of birth of every child so employed or permitted to work;

(b) hours and periods of work of any such child and the intervals of rest to which he is entitled;

(c) the nature of work of any such child; and

(d) such other particulars as may be prescribed.

12. Display of notice containing abstract of sections 3 and 14.- Every railway administration every port authority and every occupier shall cause to be displayed in a conspicuous and accessible place at every station on its railway or within the limits of a port or at the place of work, as the case may be, a notice in the local language and in the English language containing an abstract of sections 3 and 14.

13. Health and safety.- (1) The appropriate Government may, by notification in the Official Gazette, make rules for the health and safety of the children employed or permitted to work in any establishment or class of establishments.

(2) Without prejudice to the generality of the foregoing provisions, the said rules may provide for all or any of the following matters, namely:-

(a) cleanliness in the place of work and its freedom from nuisance;

(b) disposal of wastes and effluents;

(c) ventilation and temperature;

(d) dust and fume;

(e) artificial humidification;

(f) lighting;

(g) drinking water;

(h) latrine and urinals;

(i) spittoons;

(j) fencing of machinery;

(k) work at or near machinery in motion;

(l) employment of children on dangerous machines;

(m) instructions, training and supervision in relation to employment of children on dangerous machines;

(n) device for cutting off power;

(o) self-acting machines;

(p) easing of new machinery;

(q) floor, stairs and means of access;

(r) pits, sumps, openings in floors, etc.;

(s) excessive weights;

(t) protection of eyes;

(u) explosive or inflammable dust, gas, etc.;

(v) precautions in case of fire;

(w) maintenance of buildings; and

(x)   safety   of   buildings   and   machinery.

PART IV – MISCELLANEOUS

14. Penalties.- (1) Whoever employs any child or permits any child to work in contravention of the provisions of section 3 shall be punishable with imprisonment for a term which shall not be less than three months but which may extend to one year or with fine which shall not be less than ten thousand rupees but which may extend to twenty thousand rupees or with both.

(2) Whoever, having been convicted of an offence under section 3, commits a like offence afterwards, he shall be punishable with imprisonment for a term which shall not be less than six months but which may extend to two years.

(3) Whoever-

(a) fails to give notice as required by section 9; or

(b) fails to maintain a register as required by section 11 or makes any false entry in any such register; or

(c) fails to display a notice containing an abstract of section 3 and this section as required by section 12; or

(d) fails to comply with or contravenes any other provisions of this Act or the rules made thereunder.

shall be punishable with simple imprisonment which may extend to one month or with fine which may extend to ten thousand rupees or with both.

15. MODIFIED APPLICATION OF CERTAIN LAWS IN RELATION TO PENALTIES.-(1) Where any person is found guilty and convicted of contravention of any of the provisions mentioned in sub-section (2), he shall be liable to penalties as provided in sub-section (1) and (2) of section 14 of this Act and not under the Acts in which those provisions are contained.

(2) The provisions referred to in sub-section (1) are the provisions mentioned below:-

(a) section 67 of the Factories Act, 1948(63 of 1948)

(b) section 40 of the Mines Act, 1952(35 of 1982)

(c) section 100 of the Merchant Shipping Act, 1958(44 of 1958); and

(d) section 21 of the Motor Transport Workers Act, 1961(27 of 1951).

16. Procedure relating to offences.- (1) Any person, police officer or Inspector may file a complaint of the commission of an offence under this Act in any court of competent jurisdiction.

(2) Every certificate as to the age of a child which has been granted by a prescribed medical authority shall ffifor the purposes of this Act, be conclusive evidence as to the age of the child to whom it relates.

(3) No court inferior to that of a Metropolitan Magistrate or a magistrate of the first class shall try and offence under this Act.

17. Appointment of Inspectors.- The appropriate Government may appoint Inspectors for the purposes of securing compliance with the provisions of this Act and any Inspector so appointed shall be deemed to be a public servant within the meaning of the Indian Penal Code(45 of 1860).

18. Power to make rules.- (1) The appropriate Government may, by notification in the Official Gazette and subject to condition of previous publication, make rules for carrying into effect the provisions of this Act.

(2) In particular and without prejudice to the generality of the forgoing power, such rules may provide for all or any of the following matters, namely;-

(a) the term of office of, the manner of filling casual vacancies of, and the allowances payable to the Chairman and members of the Child Labour Technical Advisory Committee and the conditions and restrictions subject to which a non-member may be appointed to a sub-committee under sub-section (5) of section 5;

(b) number of hours for which a child may be required or permitted to work under sub-section (1) of section 7;

(c) grant of certificates of age in respect of young persons in employment or seeking employment, the medical authorities which may issue such certificate, the form of such certificate, the charges which may be made thereunder and the manner in which such certificate may be issued:

Provided that no charge shall be made for the issue of any such certificate if the application is accompanied by evidence of age deemed satisfactory by the authority concerned;

(d) the other particulars which a register maintained under section 11 should contain.

19. Rules and notifications to be laid before Parliament or State legislation.- (1) Every rule made under this Act by the Central Government and every notification issued under section 4, shall be laid, as soon as may be after it is made or issued, before each House of Parliament, while it is in session for a total period of thirty days which may be comprised in one session or in two or more successive sessions, and if, before the expiry of the session immediately following the session or the successive sessions aforesaid, both Houses agree in making any modification in the rule or notification or both Houses agree that the rule or notification should not be made or issued, the rule or notification shall thereafter have effect only in such modified form or be of no effect, as the case may be; so, however, that any such modification or annulment shall be without prejudice to the validity of anything previously done under that rule or notification.

(2) Every rule made by a State Government under this Act shall be laid as soon as may be after it is made, before the legislature of that State.

20. Certain other provisions of law not barred.-Subject to the provisions contained in section 15, the provisions of this Act and the rules made thereunder shall be in

addition to, and not in derogation of, the provisions of the Factories Act, 1948, the Plantations Labour Act, 1951 and the Mines Act, 1952.

21. Power to remove difficulties.- (1) If any difficulty arises in giving effect to the provisions of this Act, the Central Government may, by order published in the Official Gazette, make such provisions not inconsistent with the provisions of this Act as appear to it to be necessary or expedient for removal of the difficulty:

Provided that no such order shall be made after the expiry of a period of three years from the date on which this Act receives the assent of the President.

(2) Every order made under this section shall, as soon as may be after it is made, be laid before the Houses of Parliament.

22. Repeal and savings.- (1) The Employment of Children Act, 1938 is hereby repealed.

(2) Notwithstanding such repeal, anything done or any action taken or purported to have been done or taken under the Act so repealed Shall, in so far as it is not inconsistent with the provisions of this Act, be deemed to have been done or taken under the corresponding provisions of this Act.

23.Amendment of Act 11 of 1948.- In section 2 of the Minimum Wages Act, 1948,-

(i) for clause (a), the following clauses shall be substituted, namely:-

(a) adolescent means a person who has completed his fourteenth year of age but has not completed his eighteenth year;

(aa) adult means a person who has completed his eighteenth year of age;

(ii) after clause (b), the following clause shall be inserted, namely:-

(bb) child means a person who has not completed his fourteenth year of age;

24. Amendment of Act 69 of 1951.- In the Plantations Labour Act, 1951,-

(a) In section 2, in clauses (a) and (c), for the word fifteenth, the word fourteenth shall be substituted;

(b) section 24 shall be omitted;

(c) in section 26, in the opening portion, the words $who has completed his twelfth year shall be omitted.

25.Amendment of Act 44 of 1958.- In the Merchant Shipping Act, 1958, in section 109, for the word fifteen, the word $fourteen shall be substituted.

26.Amendment of Act 27 of 1961.- In the Motor Transport Workers Act, 1961, in section 2, in clauses (a) and (c), for the word fifteen, the word fourteen shall be substituted.

THE SCHEDULE (See section 3)

PART A- Occupations

Any occupation connected with-

(1) Transport of passengers, goods or mails by railway;

(2) Cinder picking, clearing of an ash pit or building operation in the railway premises;

(3) Work in a catering establishment at a railway station, involving the movement of a vendor or any other employee of the establishment from one platform to another or into or out of a moving train;

(4) Work relating to the construction of a railway station or with any other work where such work is done in close proximity to or between the railway lines;

(5) A port authority within the limits of any port.

(6) Work relating to selling of crackers and fireworks in shops with temporary licences.

(7) Abattoirs/slaughter Houses.

(9) Foundries;

(10) Handling of toxic or inflammable substances or explosives;

(11) Handloom and power loom industry;

(12) Mines (underground and under water) and collieries;

(13) Plastic units and fiberglass workshops;

PART B- Processes

(1) Bidi-making.

(2) Carpet-weaving.

(3) Cement manufacture, including bagging of cement.

(4) Cloth printing, dyeing and weaving.

(5) manufacture of matches, explosives and fire-works.

(6) Mica-cutting and splitting.

(7) Shellac manufacture.

(8) Soap manufacture.

(9) Tanning.

(10) Wool-cleaning.

(11) Building and construction industry.

(12) Manufacture of slate pencils (including packing).

(13) Manufacture of products from agate.

(14) Manufacturing processes using toxic metals and substances, such as, lead, mercury, manganese, chromium, cadmium, benzene, pesticides and asbestos.

(15) "Hazardous processes" as defined in Sec. 2 (cb) and dangerous operations as defined in rules made under Sec. 87 of the Factories Act, 1948 (63 of 1948).

(16) Printing as defined in Sec. 2(k) (iv) of the Factories Act. 1948 (63 of 1948).

(17) Cashew and cashew nut descaling and processing.

(18) Soldering processes in electronic industries

9) 'Aggarbatti' manufacturing.

(20) Automobile repairs and maintenance including processes incidental thereto namely, welding, lathe work, dent beating and painting.

(21) Brick kilns and Roof tiles units.

(22) Cotton ginning and processing and production of hosiery goods.

(23) Detergent manufacturing.

(24) Fabrication workshops (ferrous and non ferrous)

(25) Gem cutting and polishing.

(26) Handling of chromite and manganese ores.

(27) Jute textile manufacture and coir making.

(28) Lime Kilns and Manufacture of Lime.

(29) Lock Making.

(30) Manufacturing processes having exposure to lead such as primary and secondary smelting, welding and cutting of lead-painted metal constructions, welding of

galvanized or zinc silicate, polyvinyl chloride, mixing (by hand) of crystal glass mass, sanding or scraping of lead paint, burning of lead in enameling workshops, lead mining, plumbing, cable making, wiring patenting, lead casting, type founding in printing shops. Store type setting, assembling of cars, shot making and lead glass blowing.

(31) Manufacture of cement pipes, cement products and other related work.

(32) Manufacture of glass, glass ware including bangles, florescent tubes, bulbs and other similar glass products.

(33) Manufacture of dyes and dye stuff.

(34) Manufacturing or handling of pesticides and insecticides.

(35) Manufacturing or processing and handling of corrosive and toxic substances, metal cleaning and photoengraving and soldering processes in electronic industry.

(36) Manufacturing of burning coal and coal briquettes.

(37) Manufacturing of sports goods involving exposure to synthetic materials, chemicals and leather.

(38) Moulding and processing of fiberglass and plastic.

(39) Oil expelling and refinery.

(40) Paper making.

(41) Potteries and ceramic industry.

(42) Polishing, moulding, cutting, welding and manufacturing of brass goods in all forms.

(43) Processes in agriculture where tractors, threshing and harvesting machines are used and chaff cutting.

(44) Saw mill – all processes.

(45) Sericulture processing.

(46) Skinning, dyeing and processes for manufacturing of leather and leather products.

(47) Stone breaking and stone crushing.

(48) Tobacco processing including manufacturing of tobacco, tobacco paste and handling of tobacco in any form.

(49) Tyre making, repairing, re-treading and graphite benefication.

(50) Utensils making, polishing and metal buffing.

(51) 'Zari' making (all processes)'.

(52) Electroplating;

(53) Graphite powdering and incidental processing;

(54) Grinding or glazing of metals;

(55) Diamond cutting and polishing;

(56) Extraction of slate from mines;

(57) Rag picking and scavenging.

BIBLIOGRAPHY

Books:

➤ Alice Jacob and Kusum Kumar 'Chief Welfare', S.N. Jain, Ed. 'Child and the law' (N.M. Tripathi, 1979).

➤ Arpana Bhat Ed., *Supreme Court on Children*, (Human Rights Law Network, 2005).

➤ Asha Bajpai, *Child Rights in India: Law, Policy and Practice,* (Oxford University Press, New Delhi, 2003).

➤ Baig Tara Ali, *Our Children,* (Director Publication Division of Information and Broadcasting, Government of India, New Delhi, 1982).

➤ Burra Neera, *Born to work: Child Labour in India,* (Oxford University Press, New Delhi, 1995)

➤ B. Shiva Rao, *The Framing of Indian Constitution,* Government of India, (1966).

➤ *Child and Law,* Indian Council for Child Welfare, Chennai, Tamil Nadu, India, (1998).

➤ Dolly Singh, *Child Rights and Social Wrongs.* (Kanishka Publishers, Distributors, New Delhi, 2001).

Volume-I: *Child as victim: Dimensions of Abuse and exploitation.*

Volume-II: Violations of *Child Rights: Initiatives and Institutions for Reform.*

Volume-III: *Child as Global Citizen: A Third World Perspective.*

➤ Elias Mendelievich '*Children at Work,* (International Labour Office, 1979).

➤ Edith Abbot, *Women in Industry: A Study in America Economic History,* (New York: Appleton, 1910).

➤ *Encyclopedia of the Social Sciences,* Vol-III, Edwin R.A. Seligman, Editor-in-Chief, (Macmillan Company, 1951 reprint), p.380.

➤ New Encyclopedia Britannica Micropedia II, (15th ed. 1978)

➤ Government of India, *Encyclopedia of Social Work in India I,* (1987).

➤ Geraldine Van Bueren. *The International Law on the Rights of the Child,* (Netherland: Kluwer Academic Publishers, 1995).

- H.O. Aggarwal, *Human Rights*, (Central Law Publication Allahabad, 2003).
- Herbert A. Bloch and Frank T. Flynn, *Delinquency* New York. (Random House, 1956)
- J.C. Kulshrestha, *Child Labour in India* (Asia Publishing House, New Delhi, 1978).
- Jaswal S, *Child Labour and the Law,* (Deep & Deep Publication Pvt. Ltd., New Delhi, 2000).
- Lakshmidhar Mishra, Child Labour in India, (Oxford University Press, New Delhi, 2000).
- Leela B. Costin *Child Welfare:* Policies and Practice, McGraw Hill Book Company printed in United States of America.
- Mamta Rao, *Law Relating to Women and Children*, (Eastern Book Company, 2005).
- Manju Gupta, "*Child Labour: A Harsh Reality*", *Child Labour in India,* (1987).
- M.S. Yadav Meenakshi Bhardwaj, Learning Conditions for Primary Administration, Ministry of Human Resources, (2001).
- Narender Kumar, *Constitutional Law of India,* (Pioneer Books Delhi, 2005).
- Pauline V. Young, *Social Treatment in Probation and Delinquency,* (2nd Ed. New York: Mc. Graw – Hill, 1952).
- Rattan Lal and Dhiraj Lal, The Indian Penal Code, (Wadha and Company Law Publishers, Agra/Nagpur/New Delhi 29th ed. Reprint 2003).
- Report of Royal Commission on Labour. (Calcutta: Government of India Central Publication Branch 1931).
- Rolf Lober, David Forrengton (eds), *Serious and Violent Juvenile Offenders*, (Sage Publication Inc., 1998).
- Savities Goonesekar's *Children, Law and Justice: A South Asian Perspective*, (SAGE, 1998).
- Sutherland H. Edwin, Cressey R. Donald, *Principles of Criminology*, (The Times of India Press, Bombay, 1968).

➤ *Supreme Court on Children,* Ed. Arpana Bhat, (Human Rights Law Network, 2005).

➤ V.R. Krishna Iyer *Jurisprudence of Juvenile Justice:* A Preambular Perspective.

➤ V.R. Krishna Iyer in *'Law and Life',* (Vikas Publishing House Pvt. Ltd., Ghaziabad, 1979).

➤ Weiner Myron, *The Child and State in India,* (Oxford University Press 1991, New Delhi).

Articles/ Reports

➤ Alexander Hamilton on the employment of children: American State Paper, Documents, Legislative and Executive of the congress of the United States from the first session to the first to third session of the Thirteenth Congress, Inclusive (Washington: 1832) Class-III, France", Vol.1.

➤ Edwin R.A. Seligman, Editor-in-Chief, *Encyclopedia of the Social Sciences, Vol-III,* (Macmillan Company, 1951 reprint),

➤ Karl-Eric 'Key note address National Seminar on the rights on the child: Socio-legal perspective', 15-16 September, 1990.

➤ Shriniwas Gupta, Rights of Child and Child Labour: A Critical Study,JILI, XXXVII,(1995).

➤ *India Country Report on the Convention of the Rights of the Child,* Government of India, 1997.

➤ Annual Report, 1999-2000, Ministry of Labour, GOI

➤ G.K. Lieten, *Children Work and Education I- General Parameters,* Economic and Political Weekly, June 10, 2000.

➤ Helen Sekar, *Ensuring their childhood,* V.V.Giri National Labour Institute, New Delhi, (2001).

➤ Paras Diwan, *Child and Law,* (1980), *Position of Child under Indian Constitution,* Chandra Pal paper presented in Seminar held in Panjab University.

- Report of Royal Commission on Labour. (Calcutta: Government of India Central Publication Branch, 1931).
- Labour Investigation Committee Investigation Committee, Main Report, 1944.
- Report of National Commission on Labour, 1969
- Implementation Hand Book for the Convention on the Rights of the Child, UNICEF
- No.NI/PC/SAP/132/2000/908, dated July 31, 2000, National Institute for Public Cooperation and Child Development, GOI.
- Kartarina Tomasevski, *The Right to Education – a discussion source: International Development Cooperation Agency*

Journals and Magazines:

- All India Report
- Criminal Law Journal
- Combat Law
- Indian Journal of Public Administration
- Lawyers Times
- Journal of Indian Law Institute.
- Journal of Institute of Human Rights.
- Legal News and Views.
- UN News Letter.
- Frontline.
- Law Teller.
- Journal of Labour Legislation
- The Journal of Criminal law and Criminology
- The Lawyers
- Economic and Political Weekly

Newspaper:

- The Indian Express.
- The Tribune.

- ➢ Hindustan Times.
- ➢ The Times of India.
- ➢ The Week
- ➢ Employment News Weekly

Internet Websites:

- ➢ <http://www.bbc.co.uk>
- ➢ <http://globalmarch.org.>
- ➢ <www.hrw.org/reports/2004/india0704/4.htm#_Toc76445926>
- ➢ <http://www.ilo.org>
- ➢ <http://www.ilo.org/ilolex/cgi-lex/convde.pl?C005>
- ➢ <http://www.ilo.org/ilolex/cgi-lex/convde.pl?C007>
- ➢ <http://www.ilo.org/ilolex/cgi-lex/convde.pl?C010
- ➢ <http://www.ilo.org/ilolex/cgi-lex/convde.pl?C015>
- ➢ <http://www.ilo.org/ilolex/cgi-lex/convde.pl?C058>
- ➢ <http://www.ilo.org/ilolex/cgi-lex/convde.pl?C059
- ➢ <http://www.ilo.org/ilolex/cgi-lex/convde.pl?C112>
- ➢ <http://www.ilo.org/ilolex/cgi-lex/convde.pl?C123>
- ➢ <http://www.ilo.org/ilolex/cgi-lex/convde.pl?C138
- ➢ <http://www.ilo.org/ilolex/cgi-lex/convde.pl?R041
- ➢ <http://www.ilo.org/ilolex/cgi-lex/convde.pl?R052>
- ➢ <http://www.ilo.org/ilolex/cgi-lex/convde.pl?R096>
- ➢ <http://www.ilo.org/ilolex/cgi-lex/convde.pl?R124>
- ➢ <http://www.ilo.org/ilolex/cgi-lex/convde.pl?R146>
- ➢ <http://www.ilo.org/ilolex/cgi-lex/convde.pl?C182
- ➢ <http://www.ilo.org/ilolex/cgi-lex/convde.pl?R190
- ➢ <http://www.ilo.org/public/english/standard/relm/ilc/ilc95/pdg/rep-i-b.pdf>
- ➢ <http://www.labour.nic.in.comm2/nlc-report.html>
- ➢ <http://www.ndc-nihfw.org.html/legislation/DelhiAnti-Smoking>
- ➢ <http://www.newkerala.com/news4.php?action=full newsid=170>

- <http://www.nhrc.nic.in/Reports%20 on% 20 Trafficking.pdf>
- <http://www.ohchr.org>
- <http://timesofindia>
- <http:// www.timesofindia.indiatimes.com/articleshow/1838656.cms>
- <http://www.unicef.org>
- <http://www.unhchr.org>
- <http://www.unhchr.ch/udhr/lang/eng.htm>
- <http://www.unhchr.ch/html/menu 3/b/25.htm>
- <http://www.umn.edu/humanrts/instree/b3 ccpr.htm>
- <http://www.wcd.nic.in>
- <http://www.wcd.nic.in/crc.pdf/CRC-8.PDF>

Druck:
Canon Deutschland Business Services GmbH
im Auftrag der KNV-Gruppe
Ferdinand-Jühlke-Str. 7
00006 Erfurt